THE GREAT HOUSES OF

Natchez

THE GREAT HOUSES OF

Natchez

PHOTOGRAPHS BY

David King Gleason

TEXT BY

Mary Warren Miller and Ronald W. Miller

UNIVERSITY PRESS OF MISSISSIPPI

JACKSON AND LONDON

Publication of this book has been assisted by the generosity of the *Director's Circle of the University Press of Mississippi.*

Alcorn State University
Bookfriends of the University Press of Mississippi
Delta State University
Deposit Guaranty National Bank
Dockery Farms
Eastover Bank for Savings
Ruth and Charles Friedman
Jackson State University
Phil Hardin Foundation
John and Harriet DeCell Kuykendall
McCarty Farms
Mississippi Power Company
Mississippi Power and Light Company
Mississippi State University
Mississippi University for Women
Mississippi Valley State University
Mississippi Valley Title Insurance
Mobile Communications Corporation
Mobile Telecommunications
Norwich University
Pepsi Cola Company of Jackson
R. David Sanders
Frank E. Smith
South Central Bell
Trustmark National Bank
University of Mississippi
University of Southern Mississippi

David King Gleason expresses many thanks to Mrs. Gisela O'Brien, his studio manager who made all the reproduction prints for this book; to his associates Craig Saucier, Joe Turner, and Sarah Lyon, who backpacked equipment in and out of hospitable and warm houses in Natchez; and to his wife Josie, who was a constant inspiration for this book.

Mary and Ronald Miller gratefully acknowledge the assistance and encouragement of the Historic Natchez Foundation, Alma Kellogg Carpenter, and Dr. J. Neil Varnell.

The University Press of Mississippi thanks John S. Callon, who holds first publication rights for most of the photographs in the book, and George Scheer for his assistance in making this book a reality. The Press especially thanks the owners of the houses featured in this book.

LIBRARY OF CONGRESS CATALOGING-IN-PUBLICATION DATA

Gleason, David K.
   The great houses of Natchez.

   Includes index.
   1. Mansions—Mississippi—Natchez—Pictorial works.
2. Natchez (Miss.)—Buildings, structures, etc.—
Pictorial works. 3. Architecture, Domestic—
Mississippi—Natchez—Pictorial works. I. Miller,
Mary Warren, 1945– . II. Miller, Ronald W.,
1943– . III. Title.
NA7511.N3G54   1986   728.8'3'0976226   86-11035
ISBN 0-87805-305-0

FRONTISPIECE: Melrose

Contents

Foreword

Among those antiquarians and connoisseurs who keep track of such things, Natchez has long been famous for its prized collection of nineteenth-century architecture. For them and for all fans of historic architecture, *The Great Houses of Natchez* is a welcome look at this national treasure. While not the first attempt to capture the special quality of Natchez architecture, this volume attracts special attention by its splendid photographs aptly complemented by a text that is as reliable as it is instructive.

Every town in every state in the Union tells its unique history by the buildings and spaces which make up its physical environment. Fortune conspired to leave us precious few places that speak of history as clearly and as eloquently as Natchez. Here a tidy merchant-class town center is surrounded on three sides by magnificent suburban estates which together form a highly concentrated and well-preserved slice of nineteenth-century life in the American South. The wealth and variety of Natchez architecture would compare to eighteenth-century Williamsburg if all the great plantations strung along the James and York rivers could somehow be brought in to surround the town. In many respects the Virginia collection would still lack the remarkable integrity of Natchez architecture. On the whole, Natchez is an unrestored town where historic preservation comes quite naturally to its citizens. Perhaps the single most important factor in this preservation attitude, particularly as it concerns interiors and furnishings, is the quality of the original. The opulence of Natchez in the nineteenth century simply could not be exceeded or matched by succeeding generations. To them fell the task of caring

for and living with the taste of their ancestors even when that taste was out of fashion. Because of their careful stewardship, today Natchez can boast of the most comprehensive collection of complete and authentic interiors of any historic American city.

The story of Natchez, as told by its choicest and most famous houses, is not particularly long. It is undeniably spectacular. Consider the half century between Auburn (1812), the first "great" house in Natchez, and the forsaken shell of Longwood (1862), the ill-fated folly stopped short by the reality of war. This period is the "golden age" of Natchez architecture—a fortunate time when great wealth, social ambition, and a collective passion for living well were joined together in a remarkable series of grand houses. With their gleaming white columns, these mansions are everyman's beau ideal of a southern "plantation." Thanks mainly to Margaret Mitchell, they are heavily steeped in nostalgia—the touchstones of an irrecoverable past. *The Great Houses of Natchez* is a fresh look at these structures for what they *really* are—specimens of exemplary design and exquisite craftsmanship. By lifting the veil of nostalgia, we can quite clearly see, for instance, that Melrose (1845) is the best Greek Revival house in the South or that Lansdowne (1853) contains a carefully preserved interior worthy of admiration and serious study.

Anyone who knows Natchez knows that mansions and columns are only part of the story. Included in *The Great Houses of Natchez* is a sampling of the numerous small and medium size dwellings that dot the streetscape of town and the byways of the surrounding countryside. Some show the sophistication of

more pretentious piles—such as The Briars (1818). Others were built simply and well, with an irresistible charm that sometimes eludes their larger neighbors—examine Mistletoe for instance. Another favorite is Dr. Dubs Town House (1852), a carefully restored middle-class house engaged in something of an architectural face-off with princely Stanton Hall across High Street. Dubs seems to have purposely turned his properly dressed facade away from Stanton's conspicuous, showy front.

The undeniable appeal of Natchez architecture is self-evident. More elusive, however, have been the names of architects and builders, dates of construction or major remodelings, and other historical minutiae that form the basis of understanding in architecture. From time to time—since the 1930s at least—the domestic architecture of Natchez has been the subject of books, magazine articles, and tourist promotionals. Although some were better than others, none can be relied on for accuracy. For years folklore and genealogy have been passed off—harmlessly for sure—as architectural history. Quaint but useless references to "hand made brick," "the Spanish influence," or "petticoat mirrors" characterized many early attempts at historical journalism. Attention to historical scholarship is precisely why *The Great Houses of Natchez* is as helpful as it is handsome. The authors have distilled years of research into a thoughtful, concise introduction which examines the nature of the Natchez house, its development, design sources, and characteristics. Each house is individually introduced by a quotation gleaned from some primary source that can instruct as well as amuse (Mr. Texada's "Living Elephant," for instance). Much of this material has never been published before and greatly enhances our appreciation of the subject.

In *The Great Houses of Natchez,* we find a distinguished collection of handsome and sometimes dazzling buildings which have fascinated the architectural community for years. Professional or amateur, native or visitor, those who want to know Natchez will welcome this fresh look at the great buildings of this great town.

WILLIAM C. ALLEN
Architectural Historian
U.S. Capitol

Green Leaves

Introduction

Natchez is noted among America's historic cities for its wealth of architecturally significant buildings, preserved as evidence of the opulent life of the city's planting society during the first two-thirds of the nineteenth century. Few Southern towns have produced and then preserved such a rich architectural flowering. This outstanding achievement is made even more remarkable for its having been accomplished by a town that numbered less than 6,000 people at the time of the Civil War. The story of how and why such great architecture was produced and preserved in such a small town is found in the history of the town, its people, and its buildings.

The settlement of Natchez began in 1716 with the French establishment of Fort Rosalie, just south of the house called Rosalie that was built more than a century later. The French chose the location because it was an easily defensible position from which to protect a promising agricultural production. For defense, the fort was set atop a hill near the edge of a high cliff overlooking the Mississippi River. For farming, it was near the center of an elevated strip of extremely rich soil, well watered and healthy, that extended for a length of about 130 miles along the eastern shore of the river and for about 23 miles inland.

The fort and its surrounding settlement were known as Fort Rosalie at the Natchez, in reference to the sun-worshipping and mound-building Natchez Indians, who lived in several nearby villages. Relations between the French and Indians were fragile. In 1729, the Natchez massacred the French at Fort Rosalie; three years later, the French annihilated the Natchez as a tribe. After these tragedies, the French settlement of Natchez constituted little more than a garrison.

In 1763, the British took control as a result of the French and Indian Wars. Settlement in Natchez increased dramatically during the American Revolution, as Loyalists from the colonies sought refuge in the fertile part of what was then British West Florida. A small town was laid out at the Natchez landing in the area known today as Natchez Under-the-Hill, and large British land grants were freely given to settlers for tracts of land on top of the bluff and in the undulating countryside surrounding Natchez. In 1778, an American revolutionary named James Willing led a raid on the British in the Natchez District. The raid was unsuccessful but it served to point out to the Spanish governor of Louisiana the vulnerability of the British hold on the Natchez District.

Shortly after Spain declared war against England in 1779, the Spaniards took charge of the Natchez District despite opposition and even some incidents of open revolt. The Spanish had little impact on the language and customs of the Natchez settlers, who remained an English people under Spanish rule. However, the Spanish government had a great impact on the settlement itself by laying out the present town on the bluff in the early 1790s.

The signing of Pinckney's Treaty in 1795 ceded to America the east bank of the Mississippi River above the 31st parallel and set the stage for the end of Spanish rule in Natchez. President Washington sent Andrew Ellicott to Natchez to survey the boundary between Spanish West Florida and the United States and to establish control of Natchez. Ellicott arrived in February of 1797 and camped on the southern end of Myrtle Ridge, the present site of the House on Ellicott's Hill, where he raised the American flag in full view of the Spanish fort. Ellicott's claim on behalf of the United States had little immediate effect on the Spanish, who did not relinquish control until the following year.

Natchez became an American town in 1798, first as part of the Mississippi Territory and then, when Mississippi became the twentieth state in 1817, as part of the Union. Until the Louisiana Purchase in 1803, Natchez was especially important to the United States as the most Southwest outpost of the American government. To improve communication, a series of old Indian paths were improved to form a rude post road from Nashville to Natchez, a road that became known as the Natchez Trace. After steamboat traffic was introduced in 1811, the importance of the Trace for returning boatmen diminished, but Natchez gained in importance because of its established position as a river port. This importance grew during the first half of the nineteenth century but began to diminish with the building of railroads in the 1830s.

By the start of the Civil War in 1861, Natchez was without railroad connections and was considered by both sides to be of no strategic importance. Vicksburg, another defensible river port but connected to the rest of the Confederacy by railroads and only thirty miles or so from the state capital, was considered the prize, defended by the Confederate army and attacked by the Federals. Natchez was left defenseless, except for a group of old men, called the Silver Greys, who joined with some children in attacking a Federal gunboat stopped for ice at Natchez. The gunboat retaliated by shelling the town for three hours, killing one child.

Natchez was not defended again, either by the Silver Greys or the Confederate troops, and was quickly occupied by the Northern army after the fall of Vicksburg in 1863. Federal soldiers remained in Natchez for the duration of the war and Reconstruction.

The rise and fall of Natchez was influenced by more than the transportation routes of river, road, and rail. Other important influences were the soil, the government and its location, the healthiness of the country, and the attachment to society that was felt by the inhabitants.

The French had chosen Natchez because it was easily reached by water, was easily defensible, and was centered on an area that promised agricultural riches and a healthier, more comfortable place to live than the swamps and flatlands at other places along the river. Under the English and Spanish, Natchez capitalized on these assets and its position as the regional seat of government to attract settlers and establish its position as an important river port and settlement. Under American rule, Natchez lost the valuable government seat to more inland towns but the worth of its other resources were increased by two new developments: the invention of the cotton gin, leading to an agricultural shift from indigo and tobacco to cotton about 1795, and the inauguration of steamboat service on the river in 1811.

These new developments allowed the Natchez economy, newly based on the production and marketing of cotton, to boom. The cotton boom made Natchez politically, commercially, and culturally pre-eminent during the early nineteenth-century in the region which now includes the states of Mississippi and Alabama. Its nearest rivals on the river were Memphis and St. Louis to the north and New Orleans to the south. The Natchez merchants and planters whose fortunes were based on cotton became renowned for their opulent way of living.

The Natchez economy expanded up to the time of the Civil War despite periodic setbacks such as devastating yellow fever epidemics, the Panic of 1837, and a tornado that almost leveled the town in 1840. The largest and most long lasting setback was, of course, the Civil War and Reconstruction, which also ended

x

the period of greatest architectural significance in Natchez.

The earliest major threat to Natchez came with the gradual erosion and loss of fertility in the soil of the surrounding lands. Agricultural production shifted away from Natchez in the 1820s to plantations across the river in Louisiana and Arkansas and upriver in the broad flat lands between the Mississippi and Yazoo Rivers, an area known as the Mississippi Delta. The economy of Natchez would probably have withered if the planters had moved their families to the sites of their farming activities. However, they apparently preferred life near town to life on the plantation and continued living in Natchez, at least during the summer and fall. The planters retained Natchez as their established commercial, cultural, and social center. They amassed great fortunes from the constantly expanding cotton economy and constructed grand town houses like Stanton Hall and Magnolia Hall and magnificent suburban villas like Melrose and Longwood. These villas combined the convenience of a town house location with the serenity of a country retreat. These fine suburban estates still embrace the town like a crown of jewels and are the glory of Natchez today, just as they were in the past.

The great houses of Natchez can trace their evolution back to simple buildings. The oldest buildings, from the French and English periods, have survived only in a few published travellers' accounts that describe them as crude. One account, published in 1776, stated that Natchez had about a dozen buildings, ten of them log and two frame, all located below the bluff at the landing.

Several houses, most greatly altered, have survived from before 1800. The earliest are King's Tavern, which was built about 1794, and the central section of Richmond, which may be one of the two "wooden house[s] built in English Manner," as described in a 1786 inventory. Some others are Airlie, Hope Farm, Texada, the upper story of the Griffith-McComas House, and the House on Ellicott's Hill. These houses are for the most part simple wooden cottages, a fact often remarked upon by early visitors, who noted the predominance of wood as a building material. The

outstanding exception is Texada, identified in an 1856 newspaper description of the 1822 Audubon landscape of Natchez as the first brick house to have been built in Natchez.

Other sources of information about early Natchez architecture are drawings, government records, and travellers' descriptions. Spanish records describe floor plans that are clearly the source for the common room arrangement of the later planter's cottage. The Spanish records mention many houses with two front rooms and a back gallery that is open in the center but is closed at each end by a "cabinet" room. This same plan can be found commonly in Natchez tenant houses dating as late as the early twentieth century. Variations on the plan appear throughout the nineteenth century. One of the first changes to the early plan was the insertion of a short hall between the two front rooms, as was done at Mistletoe, Holly Hedges, and Cherokee. The resulting center hall plan is a combination of the English single pile plan with the regional device of a rear gallery between cabinets. To this variation, a room was sometimes added at each end to create a house, like the Briars and Fair Oaks, with two rooms, side by side, on each side of a central hall. This addition of end rooms produced the long, low house one room deep that was so often described as typical by early nineteenth-century travellers.

Additions could enclose and enlarge the center back gallery and make it a major room, as was done at Fair Oaks, Holly Hedges, and Cherokee. A case may even be made for the plan of Melrose, as grand as it is, deriving from that of the planter's cottage. It has a short front hall, with a room on each side, and a large center back room, with two rooms on each side, very much like a greatly enlarged version of Holly Hedges, the home the McMurrans left behind when they built Melrose.

Still another variation, close to the English double pile plan, places two rooms one behind another on each side of a central hall, but retains the center back porch flanked by "cabinet" rooms, as was done originally or as a later change at Myrtle Terrace, Twin Oaks, and Cottage Gardens.

When a building of less than two stories is arranged to follow one of these regional floor plans and is shaded by a front gallery, the building can be called a planter's cottage. The planter's cottage is a form of building that is common to Natchez, the lower Mississippi Valley, and the Gulf Coast. Its distinguishing feature is the gallery, defined as a porch that extends across the full width of a building. Joseph Holt Ingraham in his 1835 publication *The South-West. By a Yankee* noted that galleries "are as necessary to every house in this country as fire-places to a northern dwelling." These galleries provided shade from the hot sun and permitted windows to be left open for breezes during summer rains. "No house, particularly a planter's, is complete without this gallery, usually at both the back and front; which furnishes a fine promenade and dining-room in the warm season, and adds much to the lightness and beauty of the edifice," noted Ingraham.

Despite their later popularity, front galleries were not built on the earliest Natchez houses, though residents and builders soon realized their utility in combating the hot, wet Natchez climate. At first, galleries were built as shed roof additions to existing houses, producing the characteristic broken-slope gable roof. Soon, they were built as original features, retaining the shed-roof form of an addition. Eventually, they were recessed beneath the unbroken slope of a single gabled roof, like the Briars. These "undercut" or recessed galleries made the gallery a truly integral part of the structure of the Natchez house, as if the gallery were a room whose outside walls had been replaced by posts and railings.

Other architectural devices worked with the galleries to ameliorate the climate. These devices included jalousies, jib windows, and floor-length windows. Jalousies are large louvered blinds, typically used in Natchez above porch railings to admit breezes but exclude sunlight and rain. Fine examples are seen at Linden and Hope Farm. A jib window is a double-hung window with a pair of hinged panels, sometimes called jib doors, below. The earliest documented jib windows are those incorported in the building of D'Evereux in 1836. They were often added to houses

as at Elmscourt, Fair Oaks, and the Briars. When open, the jib window produced a floor-length opening that allowed greater air circulation and more direct communication between the interior and the gallery. Floor-length windows accomplish the same result but by the use of a long lower sash that extends to the floor and can be raised into the wall to make a high opening for use as a door. Floor-length windows appear to have been introduced to Natchez about 1841 at Oakland, though they are not commonly seen until the 1850s when they appear at houses like Dunleith and Stanton Hall.

The early buildings of Natchez, including the planters' cottage, were simple, straight forward and direct responses to the requirements of the climate. The buildings incorporated a mixed architectural heritage that included influences from the French, English, Spanish, and American. This melange is evident in government references to the English manner of buildings and in visitors' references to the "Chinese" plan of building. Modern attempts to classify Natchez architecture by national origin have usually proved fruitless simply because the buildings utilize many national traditions in making a local response to climatic conditions. A similar climate and mixture of national influences existed in the West Indies, where several Natchez settlers had lived and where many continued to trade. That the two areas developed a building tradition with much in common is not surprising. This similarity was noted by several visitors. The term "West Indian" is often used to describe the combination of features that characterize the architecture of Natchez, the lower Mississippi Valley, the Gulf Coast, and the islands of the West Indies.

The West Indian style is a "vernacular" rather than "academic" style. Early Natchez builders utilized a common vocabulary of architectural features, passed from builder to builder and modified to fit the client and the climate. Practicality rather than beauty ruled the production of architecture in this vernacular tradition, resulting in buildings that were usually simple and without elaborate decoration. Elaborate architectural decoration was usually part of academic architecture which is based on a study of ancient Greek

and Roman buildings. As Natchez grew, it attracted designers and builders versed in the academic architectural styles that were published in builders' guide books. Soon, builders were using academic embellishments to dress up the building forms that had been developed locally.

Early academic embellishments used in Natchez can be found on houses built of wood, like the House on Ellicott Hill which was decorated about 1800 with an apparently original fanlight over the upper front door. However, most academic details are found on houses built of brick, a more formal and costly material. The very first academic details in Natchez must include the carved cornices of Texada, built in the 1790s or around 1800 as the first brick house in town. Others were employed about 1803 at Gloucester. There, the door is crowned by a half circle fanlight with decorative curves among the radiating spines of the fan; the hand rail and newels in the stairhall are echoed on the wall by a chair rail and pilasters; and the west end is shaped in a half-octagon that is probably an original feature, repeated at the east end of the 1807 addition.

The first Natchez building to combine both the details and the form of academic architecture is Auburn, a brick building designed and built in 1812 by Levi Weeks. Weeks claimed that Auburn was the first Natchez building to use "the orders of Architecture," or the various styles of ancient Greek and Roman columns, cornices and other related elements, which are the foundation of academic architecture.

The influence of the portico at Auburn reached far beyond Natchez. It has two-story high columns and is apparently the first portico in the South to have the "big white columns" that epitomize Southern architecture. The Auburn portico predates other famous Southern examples such as the portico added to the White House in Washington and the porticoes designed by Jefferson for the University of Virginia.

A modified version of the Auburn portico was built in 1823 at Rosalie, where it is combined with other features to produce the first complete form of the grand mansions found in Natchez and, to a lesser extent, throughout the South. As introduced at Rosalie, this form is based on a nearly cubical brick block, crowned by a hipped roof with railed balustrade. Of the five openings on the front, the three center ones are sheltered by a portico supported by columns two-stories high. The columns are repeated on the rear gallery to form a colonnade extending the full width of the building.

The grand mansion form established at Rosalie was repeatedly utilized for Natchez houses up to the time of the Civil War. It was duplicated at Melrose, Homewood (burned), Choctaw, and the Harper House (demolished). It appears without the roof balustrade at Magnolia Hall and with a double-tiered rear gallery at Stanton Hall. The addition of a rear colonnade converted earlier houses like Auburn and Arlington to an approximation of the form.

The grand Natchez mansions and the planter's cottages are basic building forms that were dressed in different academic styles throughout the period before the Civil War. Each academic style combines certain distinctive features in a way that is characteristic of its particular period. The principal academic architectural styles and their periods of fashion in antebellum Natchez are: the Federal style, 1800–1840; the Greek Revival style, 1833–1870; and the Italianate style, 1855–1880.

The Federal style appears in Natchez with the earliest buildings to have academic embellishments, like Texada, the House on Ellicott Hill, and Gloucester. The style is named for the early years of the nation when Americans first adapted this style from the English neoclassical Adam style. It continued in popularity in Natchez well into the 1830s. Late examples include Glenburnie, built after the Spragues acquired the property in 1833, and Cottage Gardens, probably built or remodeled in the Federal style after about 1835.

Federal style features include oval windows, oval and half circle fanlights, delicately and deeply carved cornices and woodwork, slender Roman columns, and doors divided into six or more panels. The preferred building material was brick, laid carefully and often painted brick red with thin white lines painted in the mortar joints. Since wood was cheaper, it was the more usual building material. On unprotected exterior walls, it was applied in overlapping boards that shed rain water. On walls protected by galleries or porticoes, it was applied in the form of tongue and groove boards which produced a flat surface. The overall character of the Federal style is slender, delicate, and geometric, with emphasis on surface decoration rather than on solidity.

The Federal style was followed by the Greek Revival style—the style for which Natchez has become famous. The Greek Revival style was apparently introduced to Natchez as a fully developed style by the Agricultural Bank (now Britton and Koontz), documented to 1833. Within a few years, it had been adopted as the most popular style, but favorite Federal features continued to be employed at most otherwise Grecian buildings of the mid-1830s. The 1835 Van Court Town house has an oval fanlight and a delicate cornice, 1836 D'Evereux has oval fanlights on the back doors, and 1836 Choctaw has Roman columns and an oval window on the portico. The first purely Greek Revival residences with documented dates are Ravenna and the Burn, both under construction in 1836. The Greek Revival was the primary style until the Civil War, though it began to give way to the Italianate style in 1855.

Features of the Greek Revival style are rectangular openings, broad and flat moldings on woodwork, heavy Greek columns, and doors divided into four or two panels. The overall effect of the style was severe, bold, square, and often heavy, with an emphasis on the solidity of a building rather than its surface.

The heavy solid quality of the Greek Revival style was emphasized by the use of stucco. This favorite material of the Greek Revival style was usually grooved (and sometimes painted) to look like the blocks of stone found on ancient Greek temples. Stanton Hall, for instance, is described in 1858 as being entirely "stuccoed to a snowy whiteness" to look like marble. Where an entire exterior was not finished in stucco, stucco was usually applied to walls where they were protected by porticoes and galleries, continuing a practice that had begun during the Federal style at Rosalie and the Briars. Wooden examples in the Greek Revival style are the Burn, the Elms' 1856 wing, and Ravenna. Brick examples are Choctaw, Dixie, Melrose, and the Parsonage. Stucco was also used as a covering to update old-fashioned Federal style buildings. The 1853 remodeling of Monmouth's brick facade and the extension of Linden's wooden facade are two examples.

The construction of Monteigne in 1855 (since remodeled) documents the arrival of the Italianate style in its full blown form. The Italianate style was named for its source in Italian farmhouses as they appeared in paintings of the countryside of Italy. Features of the style are deeply overhanging eaves, bracketed cornices, half-round arches, bay windows, towers, and a continued reliance on stucco as an exterior finishing material. In Natchez, the style is often further embellished with ornamental arabesques in cast-iron.

Italianate features were incorporated into Greek Revival buildings constructed after 1855. At Stanton Hall in 1857, arched windows and an overhanging eave are found on the belvedere atop the roof and a bay window with ornamental cast-iron porch detailing is found on the side wall. Magnolia Hall, constructed after April 1858, uses the bracketed cornice on the main building and arched panels on the doors. Other buildings of the period are primarily Italianate, but include classical features. Edgewood, for instance, includes Corinthian columns as supports for its verandah and uses the old Greek Revival form for its front door.

On the eve of the Civil War, three important building projects were underway in the Italianate style, demonstrating how quickly the Italianate was promising to supplant the Greek in popular fashion. Two of these projects—the Towers and the Wigwam—involved the addition of new faces to old buildings. The third was to have been the greatest house ever built in Natchez—Longwood. Longwood, though built on an octagon plan with eclectic allusions to Oriental architecture in the arches and the onion dome, was primarily Italianate in style. Even in its unfinished state,

Longwood indicates the direction of architecture in Natchez at the onset of Civil War. Longwood silently but eloquently testifies to the impact of the Civil War on both the planting economy and the architecture of Natchez and the South.

The Civil War ruined the established economy of Natchez, but its effect on the physical aspect of the town was immediately minimal and eventually beneficial. The planting families who kept their houses had little money for remodeling. Moreover, they revered these grand reminders of life before the war. This union of no money and a reverence for the past was soon blessed by the growing awareness that the old houses were beneficial to the city. Photographs of them were often used in promotional pamphlets published between 1880 and 1920. Despite the promotional literature, Natchez grew slowly and its old residential and suburban areas looked in 1940 much the same as they had at the time of the Civil War.

This felicitous state of preservation was threatened in the 1940s when local oil strikes bolstered the economy of the town. Some remodeling and demolition did occur, but the trend was offset by the Natchez Pilgrimage, which both then and now is central to the historic preservation movement in Natchez. By the time that Natchez families had oil money to remodel their houses, ten years of the Natchez Pilgrimage had reinforced reverence for the past.

One of the first and still one of the most successful house tours in America, the Pilgrimage was initiated in 1932 by the Natchez Garden Club, some of whose members shortly thereafter formed the co-sponsoring Pilgrimage Garden Club. Today, Pilgrimage takes place twice a year, in March and October, and tourism is rapidly becoming an all-year phenomenon as more and more houses remain open throughout the year. The Pilgrimage has heightened recognition of the civic benefits of preservation by making tourism the cornerstone of the local economy.

The Natchez homeowners who share their great houses during Pilgrimage include the following individuals and organizations featured in this book:

AIRLIE
The Merrill family
ARLINGTON
Mrs. Anne Gwin Vaughan
AUBURN
City of Natchez
BANKER'S HOUSE
Mr. and Mrs. Luther Stowers
THE BRIARS
Robert Canon and Newton Wilds
THE BURN
Mayor and Mrs. Tony Byrne
CHEROKEE
Mr. and Mrs. Hugh Junkin
CHOCTAW
Mr. and Mrs. Donald DePriest
D'EVEREUX
Mr. and Mrs. Jack Benson
DIXIE
Mrs. F. N. Geddes
DR. DUBS TOWN HOUSE
Mr. and Mrs. William Carl McGehee
DUNLEITH
Mr. and Mrs. Bill Heins
EDGEWOOD
Mr. and Mrs. Richard Campbell
ELGIN
Dr. and Mrs. William Calhoun
THE ELMS
Mrs. Alma Kellogg Carpenter
ELMS COURT
Mrs. Douglas MacNeil
ELWARD
Mrs. Walter P. Abbott
FAIR OAKS
Mr. and Mrs. Bazile R. Lanneau
GLENBURNIE
Mr. and Mrs. George Guido
GLOUCESTER
Old South Society of Vedic Life

GREEN LEAVES
The Beltzhoover family
GRIFFITH-MCCOMAS HOUSE
Mrs. Charles H. Petkovsek
WILLIAM HARRIS HOUSE
Mr. and Mrs. Charles Hollingsworth
HAWTHORNE
Mr. and Mrs. Hyde D. Jenkins
HOLLY HEDGES
Mr. and Mrs. John P. O'Brien
HOPE FARM
Ethel Green Banta
HOUSE ON ELLICOTT'S HILL
Natchez Garden Club
WILLIAM JOHNSON HOUSE
United States Department of the Interior
National Park Service
KING'S TAVERN
Pilgrimage Garden Club
LANSDOWNE
The George Marshall family
LINDEN
Mrs. J. Sanders Feltus
LONGWOOD
Pilgrimage Garden Club
MAGNOLIA HALL
Natchez Garden Club
MELROSE
United States Department of the Interior
National Park Service
MISTLETOE
Mrs. Waldo P. Lambdin
MONMOUTH
Mr. and Mrs. Ron Riches
MONTEIGNE
Mrs. Hunter Goodrich
MOUNT REPOSE
Coyle Sessions Brown Trust
MYRTLE BANK
Dr. and Mrs. Thomas H. Gandy
MYRTLE TERRACE
Mr. and Mrs. Richard Durkin

OAKLAND
Mr. and Mrs. Lawrence Adams
PARSONAGE
Mr. and Mrs. Albert Metcalfe
PLEASANT HILL
Brad and Eliza Simonton
RAVENNA
Mrs. Catherine Brandon Morgan
RICHMOND
The John Shelby Marshall family
ROSALIE
Daughters of American Revolution, Mississippi
Society
ROUTHLAND
Mr. and Mrs. Charles Everette Ratcliffe
SHIELDS TOWN HOUSE
Mr. and Mrs. W. Samuel Perkins
JOHN SMITH HOUSE
Mr. Stephen A. Smith
SMITH-BONTURA-EVANS HOUSE
National Society of Colonial Dames of America,
Mississippi chapter
STANTON HALL
Pilgrimage Garden Club
TEXADA
Dr. and Mrs. George Moss
THE TOWERS
Mr. Ralph Persell
TWIN OAKS
Dr. Homer Whittington
VAN COURT TOWN HOUSE
Dr. and Mrs. Hal Ratcliffe
WEYMOUTH HALL
Mr. Gene Weber
THE WIGWAM
Mr. and Mrs. Ted Mackey

THE GREAT HOUSES OF

Natchez

AIRLIE

*Seats, Near Natchez, For Sale . . . the Real Estate of Col. John Steele, deceased, in and near said city, consisting of Belvidere, His late residence; The Cottage Place; A Cotton Farm, On the Bluff, River Bottom, covered with timber— and The Celebrated Springs, Below the Bluff. (*The Mississippi State Gazette, *September 4, 1819)*

Airlie appears to be one of Natchez's earliest houses and occupies a choice site on a high point in the northern part of town. It is a simple, unpretentious wooden dwelling that exhibits the typical form of an early planter's cottage. The house is long, low, and narrow with many doors and windows for ventilation and with a full-width front gallery for shelter from sun and rain. One indication of its early construction date is the broken slope of the gabled roof, which makes the porch look like a shed-roof addition.

Although most early Natchez houses were originally built without galleries, Natchez builders and residents soon discovered the utility of a front gallery in coping with the area's hot climate and added galleries to their houses. Another early feature of Airlie is the use of simple chamfered posts to support the gallery. Airlie's early features suggest that it is probably the "Mansion House" mentioned in an 1800 deed from Stephen Minor to John Steele. Minor was a native of Pennsylvania and an official of the Spanish government. Steele was a Revolutionary War Colonel who became secretary of the Mississippi Territory. During Steele's ownership, the house was known as Belvidere.

The name was changed to Airlie by the Aylette Buckner family, who purchased the house in 1832 and extensively remodeled the interior in the Greek Revival style. Airlie remains the home of Buckner's descendents.

ARLINGTON

VALUABLE PROPERTY FOR SALE. The estate of the late Mrs. Jane White. . . . within the limits of the City of Natchez; containing 78 acres, part of which is Woodland, on which there is an elegant two story BRICK HOUSE, *Brick Kitchen, Dairy, Stables and Carriage house, together with other out buildings. (*The Ariel, *December 26, 1825.)*

Arlington is one of the most elaborately ornamented Federal style mansions of Natchez. Its marble trim around the windows and doors, its intricately hand-carved wooden cornice, its beautifully finished and patterned brick work are all secondary to its delicate and attenuated proportions and the interaction of geometric curves that are hallmarks of the Federal style of architecture.

The enormous size of the half circle fanlights over the front and back doors, similar to published designs by New Englander Asher Benjamin, overshadows the smaller oval fanlights above the upper doors. The slender Tuscan columns of the portico are echoed by delicately reeded colonettes that support the deeply molded serpentine cornices of the front door.

On the interior, a wide and lofty center hall allows access to four separate first-story rooms, each entered through doorways surmounted by elaborately carved rectangular panels. Like many of the Natchez mansions, the stairway is located in a side hall and is entered at Arlington through a doorway with elliptical fanlight. The large parlor is furnished largely as it was when it was redecorated a decade or so before the Civil War.

Arlington was probably constructed as the residence of Mr. and Mrs. John Hampton White shortly after they acquired the property in 1818. Mrs. White, nee Jane Surget, was the daughter of Frenchman Pierre Surget who established Cherry Grove Plantation in 1788 and became the patriarch of one of the South's wealthiest planting dynasties. John Hampton White died in 1819, less than a year after acquiring the Arlington property, and his wife Jane died not long after in 1825.

Aerial view of Arlington

Auburn's outbuildings include a two-story brick kitchen to the right and an 1830s billiard hall just above the house.

Architect Levi Weeks mentioned Auburn's "geometrical staircase" in an 1812 letter.

6

AUBURN

The brick house I am building is just without the city line and is designed for the most magnificent building in the Territory. The body of this house is . . . two stories with a geometrical staircase to ascend to the second story. This is the first house in the Territory on which was ever attempted any of the orders of Architecture. The site is one of those peculiar situations which combines all the delight of romance, the pleasure of rurality, and the approach of sublimity. . . . the owner of it is a Yankey, a native of our own state, Massachusetts, and is now in Boston on a visit. His name is Lyman Harding. (Levi Weeks to Epaphras Hoyt, September 1812)

Auburn, a National Historic Landmark, was constructed in 1812 by architect Levi Weeks for wealthy attorney and planter Lyman Harding. Weeks's design for Auburn introduced academic architecture to Natchez, where the prevailing architectural character had been described as West Indian. The house is a curious mixture of the fashionable Federal style of the early 1800s and the old-fashioned Georgian style of the mid 1700s. The interior doorways with swan's neck pediments were apparently copied from an English design book dating back to 1734. However, Levi Weeks was ahead of his time in his use of the classical front portico supported by columns that are two stories tall, an influential form that became the model for later mansion houses and plantation houses throughout the South.

Auburn's portico pre-dates similar porticoes at the University of Virginia and those added in the 1820s to the White House and to Arlington in Virginia. Among the striking architectural features of the house are a free-standing spiral staircase, vaulted ceilings, an unusual T-shaped hall, and elaborately carved mantelpieces and doorways.

In 1827, Auburn was purchased by Pennsylvania native Dr. Stephen Duncan, regarded by most historians as the world's largest cotton planter in the 1850s. During Duncan's ownership, the recessed side wings were added to the main house, a two-story service building was erected to the rear, and a one-story, temple-form, frame billiard hall was built in the side yard. Other remaining outbuildings include a brick barn and a dairy house. In 1911, Duncan's heirs deeded Auburn and the surrounding acreage to the city of Natchez for use as a public park.

Both the Commercial Bank and Banker's House are similarly trimmed on the interior with large scale Greek Revival millwork and black marble mantelpieces.

BANKER'S HOUSE AND COMMERCIAL BANK

. . . The Natchez Commercial Bank are erecting a Banking House, cost $80,000, a fine massive pile on Main Street . . . (Mississippi Free Trader and Natchez Gazette, November 1, 1838.)

The Commercial Bank (now the First Church of Christ Scientist) and the Banker's House were constructed in 1838 and compose a single structure, forming an outstanding and unique expression of Greek Revival architecture. The commercial portion for banking fronts on Main Street, and the domestic portion for the residence of a bank officer faces South Canal Street. The gray marble front of the bank features a Grecian portico with colossal Ionic columns. The Banker's House is finished in stucco, scored to resemble stone, and is fronted by a classically correct Doric portico with wrought-iron railings. Both the commercial and domestic portions are similarly trimmed on the interior with large scale Greek Revival millwork and black marble mantel pieces. The architect of this National Historic Landmark complex is yet unknown, but the contractor was local builder and lumber entrepreneur Andrew Brown.

Although the bank and the Banker's House are now owned separately, the vault of the bank still occupies a first-story room beneath a second-story bedroom of the house. This arrangement allowed an officer of the bank to sleep literally on top of the money. The bank portion of the building has served Natchez as a bank, United States post office, and National Guard armory, but the First Church of Christ Scientist, who purchased the building in 1946, has enjoyed the longest continuous use. The Banker's House is now a carefully restored private residence.

THE BRIARS

The house at the Briars . . . was the residence of William B. Howell when I married his daughter, Varina, on February 26, 1845. The room in which the ceremony was performed was the front on the right of the hall entrance door.

In the winter season when the leaves have fallen off the trees it is visible from the River, and I often look at it from the steamers passing to and fro, because of the interest which attaches to it as the house in which I was married. (Jefferson Davis to W. G. Irvine, October 1889)

John Perkins, Maryland native and Natchez planter, described his residence as "That New and pleasant Situation called the Briars" when he advertised for its sale in the Natchez newspapers of 1824–25. Perkins probably built the house after he acquired the property in 1818. Today it remains as one of the most fully developed and sophisticated examples of the planter's cottage of the Lower Mississippi Valley, a long, low dwelling featuring a full-width front gallery recessed under a gabled roof. With its fanlit doorways and beautifully detailed mantel pieces, the Briars exhibits such fine Federal style woodwork that architectural historians have speculated that the house could have been designed by Levi Weeks, the architect of Auburn, before his death in 1819. The heavy timber frame of the Briars is filled with brick nogging, a construction technique of Medieval ancestry.

The Briars was rented from 1828 to 1850 to the family of William Burr Howell. In an 1845 ceremony in the parlor of the house, Howell's daughter Varina married Jefferson Davis, future president of the Confederate States of America.

The original rear gallery of the Briars was enclosed and enlarged to create a large living area elaborated by a screen of arches supported by fluted columns.

THE BURN

If you wish to see some of our work you can take a squint at John P. Walworth's House in the north part of this town. (Contractors' proposal to Jefferson College, September 29, 1837)

Situated in what were then the northern suburbs of the city, the Burn was constructed in 1836 for planter, merchant, and Natchez mayor John P. Walworth by the contracting firm of Montgomery and Keyes, who also built the West Wing and the West Kitchen at Jefferson College in nearby Washington, Mississippi. The architect was probably T. J. Hoyt, whose 1838 architectural advertisements listed as references the Burn's owner, J. P. Woolworth, and its contractor, D. Montgomery.

Hoyt chose for Walworth a Grecian design that makes it one of the earliest documented, purely Greek Revival residences in Natchez. Modestly eschewing the grand mansion house form, the owner chose to mask the two and a half stories of his large house in the form of a cottage but did not stint on fine detailing. The exterior is beautifully elaborated with paneled columns at the corners, fluted round columns on the central portico, and a complete enriched Greek Doric entablature.

A columned Grecian doorway opens onto a central hall where an unusually beautiful staircase rises along a side wall. This staircase, an outstanding architectural feature of the Burn, appears to defy gravity by turning away from the supporting wall and making an unsupported half turn as it gracefully continues to the second-story hallway. A similar staircase is found at Cottage Gardens. A rear gallery overlooks the terraced rear garden where a small brook once meandered through the property. According to oral tradition, this brook inspired Walworth to name the house the Burn, the Scottish word for brook.

The main story bedroom of the Burn is lavishly furnished in the Rococo Revival style so popular in mid-nineteenth-century Natchez.

The outstanding interior feature of the Burn is its graceful curving staircase.

CHEROKEE

Watches, Clocks, Jewelry and Fancy GOODS,—*Having now opened my large and extensive stock of New Jewelry, Watches, French Clocks and Fancy Goods, recently purchased in Europe, I would respectfully invite the attention of my friends and the public generally, to examine my goods before purchasing elsewhere, believing that in variety, style, quality and price, my stock will compare favorably with any house in or out of Natchez.* GEO. MCPHERSON. *(Natchez Daily Courier, November 22, 1855)*

Cherokee, set high above the sidewalk on a corner lot in town, is a commodious story-and-a-half house with basement. The design of the house utilizes the Greek Revival style in an unusual and sophisticated way to create an exterior of austere Grecian purity and beauty. Centered on the front of Cherokee is a bold Greek temple portico recessed between two small rooms, called "cabinet" rooms, which are more commonly found on the rear of a Natchez house but were added to Cherokee on either side of an existing portico to form a distinctive entrance. A grand entrance doorway opens onto a floor plan that is a variation on the typical Natchez arrangement of a short front hall with a room to each side and a large open room behind.

The front door is repeated at the back of the entrance hall, which opens onto a large center back room that has been enlarged to a grand scale, with floor-length windows flanking a black marble mantelpiece on the back wall. Interior millwork is executed in the robust Grecian style of the late 1830s, when the moldings still retained some of the depth of the earlier Federal style.

Cherokee, though uniform and pure in its Greek Revival finish, is the result of complicated evolution rather than a single building campaign. The exact dates and sequence of the changes are unknown. Cherokee may be an extensive remodeling of the "commodious HOUSE" advertised for sale on the lot in 1827, or it could have been built new after the introduction of the Greek Revival style to Natchez in 1833. The house sustained $3,000 damage from the May 7, 1840, tornado that nearly leveled Natchez, and its owner, David Michie, may have then remodeled or built anew.

Cherokee was owned by Frederick Stanton from 1846 until he moved to Stanton Hall in 1858. From 1861 until 1881, the family of Natchez jeweler and silversmith George McPherson occupied the house.

The rear parlor at Cherokee is a grand enlargement of a
smaller room or open porch.

CHOCTAW

For Sale. THAT *large three-story Brick House, situated on the corner of Wall and High streets, on a lot of ground 160 feet square on each street. The House contains 10 rooms above the basement, 8 of which have elegant marble mantels. The rooms are large and airy. The basement contains five or six rooms—a Stable and Carriage House are on the lot, with shrubbery and trees—making it a very handsome and desirable residence for a large family. . . .* ALVAREZ FISK. (The Daily Courier, *November 26, 1852.)*

Choctaw was built in 1836 as the residence of contractor and real estate investor Joseph Neibert, who in partnership with Peter Gemmell, operated a large contracting business in antebellum Natchez. The house has long been attributed to architect and builder James Hardie, who served as superintendent of construction for Neibert and Gemmell when the house was built.

Like D'Evereux and the Van Court Town House, the house was built during the transition period in Natchez from the Federal to the Greek Revival style and has architectural details characteristic of each style. The portico is Federal and features Roman Ionic columns and an oval light in the pediment, but the entrance doorway and interior millwork are Greek. On the interior, folding doors separate the short front hall from the two front rooms. In the wider back hall, a flight of stairs follows a curved wall to form a graceful half oval as they rise first to the second floor and then continue to a third-story large room, which is lighted by a band of windows high on the wall.

In 1844 Choctaw became the home of Alvarez Fisk, a wealthy planter of Natchez and New Orleans. Fisk was a philanthropist who gave the city of Natchez the property for the Natchez Institute, the first public school in Mississippi to offer a full course of free education. Choctaw probably received its name after it was acquired in 1855 by George Malin Davis, since Fisk referred to the house as "The Hall."

From the top, Cherokee, Choctaw, city auditorium (1940), and the House on Ellicott's Hill.

Built during the transitional period from the Federal to the
Greek Revival style, Choctaw has a Federal style portico and
18   a Grecian doorway.

COTTAGE GARDENS

*It is with heartfelt sorrow that the Democrat this morning announces the death of Capt. A. H. Foster, one of the city's oldest and most greatly beloved citizens. . . . There are probably few of the present generation who realize the wonderful service rendered by Capt. Foster to this community during the dark days of reconstruction. . . . [He] exercised a wonderful influence over the carpet-baggers as well as the emancipated [Negro] . . . and this influence was in great measure responsible for this section not passing through the same baptism of fire and blood that was so prevalent in practically every other section. (*The Daily Democrat, May 18, 1919.)

Cottage Gardens is a story-and-a-half wooden cottage that combines the typical Natchez gallery, recessed under the unbroken slope of a gable roof, with a triangular pediment, more usually associated with a projecting portico. This rare combination is not found as an original feature at any other Natchez house. The original front porch columns, made of solid logs squared off in the Greek Revival style, were replaced in the 1960s with the present round columns. Connecting the columns is a "sheaf-of-wheat" pattern railing like that installed at Choctaw about 1836.

Another architectural feature common to both Choctaw and Cottage Gardens is the sunburst-pattern oval window that lights the pediment. Cottage Gardens also had a recessed back gallery, originally open across the full width of the house but later enclosed at each end by the early addition of two "cabinet" rooms.

The interior trim consists of door and window casings with simple Grecian backbands, a mantelpiece with a broad frieze supported by bold Greek Doric columns, and a superb staircase that is a near mate for the 1836 staircase original to the Burn.

Cottage Gardens probably achieved its present form during the 1830s or 1840s. The house may have been built new at that time or it may have been a thorough remodeling of an earlier house. From 1845 to 1867, Attorney Josephus Hewitt lived in the house, which he called "Glen Home." In 1884, Cottage Gardens became the home of the Allison Foster family, who gave the house its present name and resided there until 1963. Allison Foster had come to Natchez as a Union army officer in 1863. He married a Natchez girl and became one of the city's most beloved and respected citizens.

D'EVEREUX

To Day Our City was visited by the Hon. Henry Clay, he came soon after breakfast, The reception was rather cold for a Community to have been so Long apprised of his near Approach to Our City, . . . After a Stay of an hour or so he was then taken Out in a Carriage drawn by a pr of fine Bay Horses to the Residence of Mr St John Elliotte where He Dined &c (William Johnson's Natchez: The Ante-bellum Diary of a Free Negro, *December 6, 1842)*

D'Evereux was built for William St. John Elliott, probably shortly after he bought the property in 1836. Although D'Evereux is considered one of the monuments of Greek Revival architecture, its Federal style fanlighted rear doorways testify to its construction during the mid-1830s period when Natchez builders were changing from the Federal to the Greek Revival style. Local tradition has long credited the design of the house to Natchez architect and builder James Hardie. Elliott is supposed to have named the house for his mother's brother, General John D'Evereux, who served with Simon Bolivar.

A native of Maryland, William St. John Elliott became a wealthy Natchez planter noted for his philanthropy. Elliott died childless in 1855 and left behind a will with an unusual stipulation. At the death of his wife, "D'Evereux Hall," as it was once called, was to become the property of his nephew, William St. John Elliott Parker, "with this proviso—that the said Parker recovers his health and takes on my name alone and by legislative sanction—so as to represent me as my son—should he however prefer to wear the name he has— why then I give and bequeath D'Evereux Hall to a Male Catholic Orphan Asylum to be incorporated by the legislature under the style of D'evereux Hall Orphan Asylum." Although the nephew did not comply with the terms of the will, Elliott's widow managed to circumvent the will and retain D'Evereux as her family's home by endowing the construction of D'evereux Hall Orphan Asylum in Natchez.

D'Evereux's rear gallery overlooks a terraced garden that was once flanked by matching, two-story brick dependencies, one of which survives.

D'Evereux's dining room, like the rest of the interior, has a domestic scale and is beautifully ornamented with marble mantelpiece and plaster cornice and frieze.

DIXIE

By virtue of a decree of the Probate Court, rendered on the 22nd day of January 1855, the undersigned will expose to sale, at public auction . . . the estate of the late Edward R. Templeman, deceased, to-wit: That new, spacious and beautiful Brick Dwelling at the corner of Wall and Washington streets, in the City of Natchez. The building is well adapted to the accommodation of a genteel family, and has never been occupied since completion. (Probate Box 156—Estate of Edward Templeman)

Bachelor Edward Templeman had begun the construction of Dixie by June 1, 1853, when he complained to the city of Natchez about the high tax assessment on his property, considering that the house was still under construction. The high valuation is understandable today, however, for Dixie, though a small brick cottage, boasts an expansive stately air that is largely the result of its imposing Greek Doric portico.

This porch, like a Grecian temple, is subtly emphasized by the contrast between the warm rose brick walls and the scored stucco central section behind the portico.

The small, geometric front garden is similar to those at other antebellum Natchez town houses that were built close to the street. On the interior, a central passageway is flanked by double rooms. The stair to the two upstairs rooms is located in an enclosure to one side of the back hall.

For many years in this century Dixie stood unoccupied and neglected. The roof was open to the weather and the floors had rotted and fallen in. Most people in Natchez thought Dixie had deteriorated beyond salvage until restored mid-century by Tom Ketchings.

DR. DUBS TOWN HOUSE

Dr. Charles H. Dubs, Dental Surgeon, corner of Pearl and High streets, Natchez, With many and sincere thanks to the generous citizens of Natchez and the surrounding country, whose patronage he has so liberally received, respectively announces to the public that he still continues to give his undivided attention to DENTAL SURGERY *in all its various branches, aided by many valuable improvements together with the constant practice of fifteen years in this city. Office at his residence, southeast corner of the above streets.* (The Daily Courier, *April 19, 1855*)

Philadelphian Dr. Charles H. Dubs, Natchez alderman and dentist, built his Greek Revival townhouse in 1852. He chose for his house a severely rectilinear form, like that of a Northern town house, and relied for decorative effect upon the quality of its workmanship. The brickwork of the front wall, which retains its original mortar, is outstanding. The bricks are laid with finely shaped mortar joints in an all stretcher bond with no brick ends visible. The restored original decorative painting scheme of the interior features graining and marbleing on all interior trim except for door and

window surrounds. The original decorative painting may be the work of ornamental painter J. N. Charlesworth, who was recommended by Dr. Dubs in a newspaper advertisement of 1854. In 1854 Dubs added a rear wing and a small, two-story outbuilding, after which he began to advertise that both his office and his residence were located in the house. Scratched into the brick of the front section of the house is "Built 1852." The rear wing bears the inscription, "1854/Built by C. H. Dubs/1854."

DUNLEITH

As Mr. Routh increased his worldly store he added to and raised his house to a two-story building, with columns and upper galleries on two sides, as which it remained until about thirty years ago, when it was struck by lightning and destroyed, in consequence of my wife desiring terra cotta chimney tops placed, which were elevated above the surrounding china trees, and so affording an object for the electric fluid. I rebuilt the house after a plan by Mr. A. J. Downing, carried out by Mr. [John] Crothers, one of the best and ablest mechanics, and which barring accident, will long remain as evidence of his skill and fidelity, for no more substantial house was ever erected, and although the name has been changed by some of the owners through whose hands it has passed, yet the original name of "Routhland" should be restored in order to commemorate one of the historical landmarks of the olden time. (Charles G. Dahlgren, letter to The Daily Democrat, *January 24, 1886)*

A National Historic Landmark, Dunleith is the only house in Mississippi that is completely encircled by a colossal colonnade.

Constructed in 1856, the great house was the in-town villa of Mr. and Mrs. Charles Dahlgren. Located atop a rise on the edge of a forty-acre landscaped park within the original city limits of Natchez, Dunleith boasts an array of outbuildings associated with antebellum life on a suburban estate. These outbuildings, several of which are built in the style of a Gothic castle or fort, include a three-story service wing with antebellum bathroom, a two-story poultry house, a two-story carriage house and stable, and an original hothouse for the garden.

Dunleith is the name given the house about the time of the Civil War by its second owner, Alfred Vidal Davis. The Dahlgrens had called the house Routhland, the name of Mrs. Dahlgren's family home that had stood on the same site until its destruction by lightning in 1855. The builder of Dunleith was Maryland native John Crothers, who employed Italianate details to enliven the basic Greek Revival style.

Although Dahlgren asserted that A. J. Downing designed Dunleith, Downing's death three years before the earlier Routhland burned and Downing's contempt for the Greek Revival style suggest that Dahlgren confused A. J. Downing with his contemporary A. J. Davis, who was a major published architect in the Greek Revival style. It is possible, however, that Downing's influence is reflected in the design of the outbuildings, which are similar to those published by Downing in the *Architecture of Country Houses.*

Dunleith is surrounded by a forty-acre landscaped park and boasts an array of outbuildings that include a three-story service wing, poultry house, carriage house, and hot house, three of which are in Gothic style.

EDGEWOOD

—Specifications—for the erection of a Country Residence— for—Saml. H. Lambdin Esqr./Howard & Diettel Architects/New Orleans Feb. 25th 1859.

Mechanics Lien/Samuel H. Lambdin, Esq. To Thomas Rose, Dr./1860 April 10/For Carpenters work on new dwelling— furnishing plank for doors, sash and blinds: moldings for doors. . . . /$8,500.00. (Adams County Deed Book NN:611)

Edgewood is one of the finest Italianate style buildings in the Natchez vicinity and was begun in 1859 as the residence of Samuel H. Lambdin and his wife, the former Jane Bisland of Mount Repose. An 1853 letter to Samuel Lambdin from his brother James Reid Lambdin, a noted Philadelphia portrait artist, indicates that the Natchez Lambdins had been searching for a suitable house site for several years before construction began. The house was finally built on a portion of Mount Repose and derives its name from its location at the southeast edge of the property. Edgewood was designed by the noted New Orleans architectural firm of Howard & Diettel, which also designed Nottoway on the River Road in Louisiana. The local builder was Thomas Rose, who was the builder and possibly the designer of Stanton Hall in Natchez.

Unlike most of the great Natchez mansions, Edgewood has its staircase as the focal point in the central entrance hall of the house. The house also originally featured such modern devices as a speaking tube and inside plumbing for lavatories in upstairs bedrooms. A winter kitchen was located in the partially raised basement of the house and a summer kitchen was provided by a nearby outbuilding.

The spacious interior of Dunleith is richly trimmed with ornamental plaster and marble mantel pieces. Windows are floor-length to provide complete access to the encircling galleries. (*left*)

Unlike most Natchez mansions, Edgewood's staircase is the focal point of its grand hallway. (*right*)

Edgewood is entered by its original drive, which has become depressed through use and is now enclosed by high banks. (*left*)

Edgewood is an Italianate suburban villa residence designed in 1859 by Howard and Diettel of New Orleans. (*right*)

ELGIN

Mrs. Dr. Jenkins . . . died of yellow fever yesterday. She was a shining mark for death's arrow—so lovely one could hardly suppose it possible that so loathsome a disease could have found access to her. (Diary of Reverend Joseph Buck Stratton, September 17, 1855)

Attended in the afternoon the funeral of Dr. John C. Jenkins of "Elgin" near Natchez; . . . Less than a month ago we buried Mrs. Jenkins. Her husband stood by her grave, now he lies where he then stood. (Stratton, October 14, 1855)

Elgin is a broad but shallow house, five rooms across but only one room deep, that allows each room full access to cool breezes and to shade afforded by a generous full-width gallery set beneath the protection of a gable roof. Elgin gains distinction from its two-story height and double-tiered gallery, which grace the plantation house with a beauty that is imposing and serene. Jib windows, or windows set above hinged panels, allow unlimited access from the rooms to both levels of the gallery.

This modest but expansive expression of the Greek Revival style was created between 1840 and 1855 by Dr. John Carmichael Jenkins, a Pennsylvania native who came to Natchez, married the granddaughter of William Dunbar, wealthy planter and amateur scientist, and established himself at Elgin as a planter, a medical doctor, and a nationally known horticulturalist.

Dr. Jenkins's horticultural experiments and the construction of his house are well documented in his detailed plantation diary. In 1840, Dr. Jenkins purchased Elgin Plantation, on which was standing a small, Federal style, one-story residence that had earlier been the residence of his wife's uncle, Archibald Dunbar. Shortly after he acquired the house, Dr. Jenkins built a two-story addition that was one room deep with a center hall dividing two rooms on each floor. In 1851 he extended the two-story section the depth of one room at the eastern end, and, in 1855, he added a matching addition to the western end. In 1853 Jenkins built an impressive two-story brick kitchen building with giant order (two stories tall) columns. In 1855 both Dr. and Mrs. Jenkins died during one of the city's most devastating yellow fever epidemics.

Elgin's double-tiered gallery graces the plantation house with a beauty that is imposing and serene. To the right is the brick kitchen building built by Dr. Jenkins in 1853.

Dr. Jenkins remarked in an 1840 letter that a "local wag" had described his new addition to Elgin as making the old house look like the "amen at the end of a long prayer." (*left*)

33

THE ELMS

The subscriber will sell the House and Lot on which he now resides, for Cash or Cotton. There is about 11 acres attached to the Lot—the Buildings and Fences are nearly new—the situation allowed to be as agreeable as any in the Town or vicinity of Natchez. John Henderson. (Natchez Chronicle, April 30, 1810)

The Elms is one of the earliest documented houses in Natchez and is the result of at least three distinct building stages that have combined to produce a residence that is one of the most picturesque eclectic dwellings in the entire South. The house was constructed ca. 1804 in the Federal style as the residence of John Henderson, a Scotchman who immigrated to Natchez in 1787 and wrote the first book published in the Natchez territory. Henderson purchased the property in 1804 and described the house as "nearly new" when he advertised it for sale in 1810.

The Elms was originally a two-and-a-half story brick house with two rooms on each floor. Not long after the house was built, the rear two-story gallery was enclosed and eventually double-tiered galleries were constructed to encircle completely the enlarged house.

The last major renovation occurred in the 1850s during the ownership of David Stanton, brother of Frederick Stanton of Stanton Hall. A two-story, Greek Revival, stuccoed-frame wing was added to the front porch of the house, and the porch was enclosed to serve as an entrance hall. Stanton's 1850s renovation changed the way the house faced from south to west and it included the construction of a Greek Revival billiard hall in the side yard. The Elms has been carefully preserved by succeeding generations of the Drake family since 1869.

The circular cast-iron staircase was installed as the focal point of a new entrance hall created in the 1850s remodeling. The Rococo Revival parlor furniture was brought to the Elms by the Drake family in 1869 and retains its original wool plush upholstery. (*left*)

34

ELMS COURT

To the north and east of "Longwood" and "Gloster" on the Liberty Road was "Elmscourt," the handsome home of A. [P] Merrill, who was considered a Union man. At any rate, some of his property was destroyed by Confederates and on one occasion a detail was sent by the Confederate General Wirt Adams to burn his residence, but they were driven off. The Merrills were an interesting and accomplished family. After the war, General Grant sent Mr. Merrill to Brussels as our minister. (Matilda Gresham, wife of the Union commander of the occupation of Natchez, Life of Walter Quintin Gresham *1832–1895, 1919)*

Elms Court, situated in the midst of a wooded and landscaped park, is one of the most outstanding suburban villa residences of Natchez. The construction of the two-story center portion of the Greek Revival mansion was probably begun in 1836, when the property was acquired by Eliza and Catherine Evans. These two women were daughters of prominent contractor Lewis Evans, whose will stipulated that they were to receive three thousand more dollars than their sisters to be invested in a permanent property.

In 1852 the house was purchased by wealthy planter Francis Surget, who presented the house as a wedding present to his daughter Jane and her husband Ayres P. Merrill, both natives of Natchez. During the 1850s, the Merrills added the one-story side wings, replaced the original portico with a double-tiered, cast-iron railed gallery, and richly remodeled the interior of the house. Like many of the wealthy Natchez planters, Ayres P. Merrill was opposed to secession and was rewarded for his loyalty to the Union by being appointed ambassador to Belgium by President Grant in 1876.

In 1895 James Surget of Cherry Grove Plantation acquired Elms Court from his Surget relatives and gave the house as a wedding present to his daughter Carlotta and her husband David McKittrick, whose descendants still occupy the house. Elms Court, whose lavish ornamental ironwork is arranged in galleried tiers like a wedding cake, was twice given as a wedding present to daughters of the Surget family.

The punkah, or fly fan, suspended over the dining table at Elms Court, has a wooden frame originally covered in painted canvas. (*right*)

The plaster ceiling centerpiece of Elms Court's entrance hallway is finely executed and has unusual depth.

The architectural evolution of Elms Court is illustrated in an aerial photograph.

ELWARD

RICHARD ELWARD, *Book-binder in Natchez, is an accomplished workman. . . . He equals New York on blank books, and we commend him to the whole state.* (Weekly Courier and Journal, *June 24, 1840)*

Elward was constructed about 1844 as the residence of Richard Elward, a book-binder and Natchez newspaper editor. Set close to the street on a corner lot encircled by a palisade fence, the brick cottage is distinguished by the high quality of its exterior, Greek Revival woodwork. Like other Greek Revival brick cottages in Natchez, the house features gable-end chimneys linked by a brick wall that extends above the roof.

The upper half-story is lighted by two original dormer windows, trimmed with pilasters and cornice, that are set on either side of a narrow central dormer that is a later addition. An original railing of narrow, turned balusters links the two Grecian box columns of the portico with their matching pilasters on the front wall. The entrance doorway is set in a peaked enframement with elaborately decorated sidelights and transom. The decoration of the sidelights and transom is achieved by facing square panes of glass with strips of wood bent to form hollow-sided diamonds.

FAIR OAKS

*On nearly every piazza in Mississippi may be found a wash-
stand, bowl, pitcher, towel, and water-bucket, for general
accommodation. . . . Here they wash, lounge, often sleep,
and take their meals.—Here will the stranger or visitor be
invited to take a chair, or recline upon a sofa, settee, or form,
as the taste and ability of the host may have furnished this
important portion of a planter's house. I once called on a
planter within an hour's ride of Natchez, whose income
would constitute a fortune for five or six modest Yankees. . . .
The planter was sitting upon the gallery, divested of coat,
vest, and shoes, with his feet on the railing, playing, in high
glee, with a little dark-eyed boy and two young negroes,
who were chasing each other under the bridge formed by
his extended limbs. (Joseph Holt Ingraham,* The South-
West. By a Yankee, *1835)*

The great length and high finish of the gallery at Fair Oaks
render the house an outstanding illustration of the Mississippi planter's house described in Joseph Holt Ingraham's
1835 *South-West. By a Yankee.* The gallery is deep and long
enough to accommodate the outdoor living requirements of
a large family. Because the gallery at Fair Oaks is just as important as any room in the house, it is made an integral part
of the structure, set beneath the main roof as if it were a
room whose walls have been replaced by slender columns
and open railings. The gallery is trimmed as finely as an interior room, with baseboard, chair rail, and paneled wain-
scot. The hinged panels beneath the windows, called jib
windows, increase ventilation and allow easy access between
rooms of the house and the gallery.

   The original house was only one room deep with a rear
gallery whose ends were enclosed by small cabinet rooms.
Two rooms are located on each side of a room-size entrance
hallway with fireplace. The beautifully detailed, Federal
style fanlight of the entrance doorway is repeated at the back
of the center hall and between the hall and parlor. The floor
plan of the house was elaborated by the early addition of a
dining room at the back of the center hall. Although documents suggest that a house was on the property in 1822, the
broadness of the moldings indicate that the Fair Oaks millwork dates as late as the early to mid 1830s. In 1856 the
property was purchased and named Fair Oaks by Dr. Orrick
Metcalfe, whose descendants still occupy the house.

The dining room of Fair Oaks is an early addition accessed
through a fanlighted doorway at the back of the entrance
hall. The shape of the ceiling punkah, or fly fan, suggests a
hoopskirted woman. (*left*)

GLENBURNIE

The well known residence of the late Col. Sturges Sprague is offered for sale with all the valuable property attached thereto. It is conveniently situated about a mile and half from Natchez and is generally considered to be one of the most desirable residences in the vicinity of Natchez. The dwelling House is a new and commodious edifice, all the requisite buildings, stables, &c., are in complete order. The situation for health or pleasantness is unrivalled. (The Weekly Courier and Journal, *January 22, 1840)*

Glenburnie was built as the residence of attorney Sturges Sprague and his wife Frances on property she acquired in 1833. The Spragues probably built their Federal style house the same year that construction of the Agricultural Bank (now Britton and Koontz Bank) introduced the Greek Revival style to Natchez. The house exhibits the typical form of the Mississippi planter's cottage—a single-story dwelling with a full-width gallery recessed beneath the slope of the gabled roof. The roof is supported by delicate turned columns like those at the Briars and Fair Oaks. A fanlighted center doorway opens into a short front hall with a room on each side and a larger room behind. A sympathetic and significant Colonial Revival addition with galleries was made to the house by Mr. H. G. Bulkly about 1901. An early twentieth-century publication described Glenburnie as "a most attractive villa, with a wide sweeping lawn in front" that has been "added to by Mr. Bulkly's taste and wealth."

Glenburnie attracted national attention in 1932 as the scene of the murder of Miss Jennie Merrill. Dubbed the "Goat Castle Murder" by the press, the crime exposed to a curious nation the eccentric lifestyles of members of several prominent Natchez families. The prime suspects were Dick Dana and Octavia Dockery, later proved innocent, who were living in squalor with chickens and goats at the neighboring antebellum mansion, Glenwood.

GLOUCESTER

Proceeding to the southward from Natchez, I passed some tasty cottages, and deviating a little to the right of the main road, in two short miles I came to the colonel (late governour) Sargent's handsome brick house. The road led through a double swinging gate into a spacious lawn, which the colonel had formed in the rear of the house, the chief ornament of which was a fine flock of sheep. The appearance of his plantation bespoke more taste and convenience than I had yet observed in the territory. (Fortescue Cuming, Sketches of a Tour to the Western Country, *1810)*

Gloucester is a unique architectural achievement, based on a complicated series of changes that incorporated several local building traditions and raised them to new heights of sophistication. At Gloucester, the floor plan of the planter's house, one room deep with cabinet rooms, has been combined with the form of the Natchez mansion, with its colossal-columned front portico and rear gallery. This combined form is executed with half octagon ends, a dry moat, a "U" shaped hall, and paired front doors to produce a delightful and handsome house like no other in the nation.

Gloucester is a broad two-story brick house with tall Tuscan columns supporting the wide portico. The portico shades two matching front doors with the half-round fanlights and the separate sidelights associated with the earliest houses of Natchez. Across the back is a large colonnaded gallery, closed at each end by cabinet rooms. A brick-lined dry moat lights and ventilates the full basement. Gloucester is three rooms across, with the parlor on the west and the dining room on the east. In the center is a smaller room and a front cross hall connecting two matching stairhalls.

Gloucester was constructed after the property was acquired by Samuel Young in 1803. Originally called Bellevue, the house was purchased in 1807 by Winthrop Sargent who renamed it "Gloster Place" in honor of his Massachusetts birthplace. Sargent had come to Natchez in 1798 to serve as the first governor of the Mississippi Territory. Sargent's papers indicate that he built the eastern addition, consisting of the dining room, east stair hall, and rooms above and below, immediately after purchasing the house. This addition was suggested to Sargent by his friend Lyman Harding, also from Massachusetts, and by Harmon Blennerhasset, who came to Natchez with the Aaron Burr expedition in 1807. The two-story portico and front cross hall were added later to help create one of Natchez's most historically and architecturally significant mansions.

The Gloucester dining room with its semi-octagonal end wall was built as an early addition in 1807.

The outstanding interior feature of Gloucester is the U-shaped hallway with two staircases and richly molded arches elaborating the front hall section, which opens into the two end rooms through fanlighted doorways.

GREEN LEAVES

E. P. Fourniquet, Esq. is finishing an elegant wooden dwelling house, corner of Washington and Rankin streets, at a cost of $25,000. This house is in a new style of shape and finish, which, will, if we mistake not, be extensively adopted in the South. The two ranges of double parlors, divided by a spacious hall, connecting with the front and rear balconies; the sitting rooms and cabinets in the wings of the building; with the dining room and offices in the basement,—present convenience connected with compactness and architectural beauty. (Mississippi Free Trader and Natchez Gazette, November 1, 1838)

Green Leaves was constructed in 1838 as the residence of Edward P. Fourniquet and is one of the most richly detailed Greek Revival houses in Natchez. An enriched Doric portico shelters the entrance doorway which opens into a lavishly trimmed hallway. The four doorways of the central hall are framed by flat columns or pilasters supporting overhanging cornices, all richly molded.

Green Leaves is one of the great Natchez houses where succeeding generations of a single family have carefully preserved important architectural and interior decoration dating to before the Civil War. In 1849 the house was purchased by George W. Koontz who, in partnership with William and Audley Britton, established Britton and Koontz Bank, still a major financial institution in Natchez. Descendants of George W. Koontz still occupy Green Leaves, and their careful preservation of the house and its Empire and Rococo Revival furnishings makes it one of America's most valuable documents of mid-nineteenth-century taste. These important interior furnishings include curtains, gilt cornices, wall-to-wall carpeting, wallpaper, and furniture.

The rear courtyard of Greenleaves is shaded by a massive live oak tree and is enclosed on three sides by the rear gallery of the house and the galleries of the flanking rear wings.

GRIFFITH MCCOMAS HOUSE

Our attention was called a day or two since, to an old and most interesting picture belonging to, and now hanging in the store of Mr. Emile Profilet. It was painted by the elder Audubon, the celebrated Ornithologist, in 1822. It represents Natchez in the olden time. . . . it will recall to the minds of all our old residents the familiar scenes of younger days. . . . In some cases . . . a basement story has been built underneath the former wooden edifice; but, in most cases, the old tenements have given place to new and spacious stores and buildings. (The Natchez Daily Courier, *March 7, 1856*)

The wooden upper story of the Griffith McComas House is almost certainly the "tenement house" that was standing on this lot in 1818. It may have been built for Hugh Coyle, a tailor who owned the land from 1793 to 1799, or for Leonard Pomet, a shopkeeper who owned the lot from 1799 to 1807.

The asymmetrical arrangement of the doors and windows in the upper frame story is typical of late eighteenth and early nineteenth-century buildings of the region. Within a few decades of its construction, the wooden story was jacked up and placed on a new brick first story, a common practice in early nineteenth century Natchez. The symmetry of the openings on the front of the new lower story is typical of the Federal style, which was popular in Natchez from about 1800 to about 1836. Also in the Federal style is the first-story entrance, beautifully elaborated with an elliptical fanlight, sidelights, and four slender columns. The columns of the doorway are echoed on an interior mantel piece, which is further decorated by ovals carved in a sunburst pattern.

The present front gallery is a 1960s reconstruction of the original that was lost to a Victorian renovation. The house received its name from William and John Griffith, who owned the house from 1819 to 1830, and from General J. H. McComas's widow, Anna, who purchased the house in 1851.

Double parlors at Green Leaves

WILLIAM HARRIS HOUSE

This community lost by death yesterday one of its oldest and most respected citizens when Mr. N. L. Carpenter, in the 87th year, entered into his eternal rest. Mr. Carpenter was one of the few venerable links that bound the present to a past generation, and who, although outliving but few of his contemporaries, was an active and interested citizen in all affairs of this community. . . . Mr. Carpenter was born in the State of Vermont, but came to Natchez in his early manhood where he has continued to reside, and where the evidence of his energetic and useful life remain to bear the impress of his enterprise. He was the founder of the Natchez batting mill, was largely interested in the oil works and the Natchez Cotton Mills. . . . The Democrat *renders to his afflicted family its deepest sympathy, and recognizes the loss our community has sustained in the fall of this brave old oak that has withstood the storms so many years in monumental sturdiness. (*The Daily Democrat, *December 24, 1892)*

The William Harris House is an imposing two-story house set close to the sidewalk in downtown Natchez. The first story of the house is brick and the second story is frame— a form of house called a "double house" in a nineteenth-century building contract. The basic shape and most of the interior Greek Revival trim is original to the mid-1830s, when the house was built. Exterior elaborations like the bay window on the western side, the Grecian front doorway, and the double-tiered portico were probably added after an 1855 fire severely damaged the house. The columns and railings are like those documented as original to the 1860 Shields Town House. On the interior, a central hall with two rooms on each side leads to a back gallery that originally had cabinet rooms at each end.

The William Harris House was built about 1833 to 1835. Harris was an alderman, commission merchant, planter, and real estate developer. In 1835 and 1836, he was building Ravenna for his family home. In 1851 the house was purchased by Nathaniel Loomis Carpenter, who the same year sold Myrtle Terrace to steamboat captain T. P. Leathers. A builder by trade, Carpenter probably supervised the ca. 1855 elaborations to the exterior. Carpenter amassed a fortune in his lifetime and was the patriarch of Natchez's most philanthropic family. The Carpenter family sold the house in 1886, by which time they had already purchased Dunleith, their family home for five generations.

HAWTHORNE

Mas. R Dunbar requests the pleasure of your company on Friday evening at five o'clock. Hawthorne, Jan 4th 1843. (Invitation to Master Henry Quitman)

MARRIED . . . *At Hawthorne, near Natchez, on Thursday, 27th inst, by the Rev. Wm. R. Babcock, JAMES R. CURELL of New Orleans, to VIRGINIA C. daughter of Mrs. R. Dunbar of Natchez. (*Natchez Weekly Courier, *May 3, 1854)*

Hawthorne is a Federal style house distinguished by the marked contrast between the small scale of its cottage-like exterior and the grand scale of its interior spaces. High ceilings, large rooms, broad center halls, and beautifully carved Federal style mantelpieces are notable features of the spacious interior, but the four doorways with matching elliptical fanlights are outstanding. These doorways are located at the front and rear of the house and on either side of the front hall. A fifth elliptical arch, resting on turned columns, separates the shorter front hall from the wider back stair-hall. The heavy frame construction of the house is made even stronger by the use of brick nogging, a form of building found in Medieval England and early America. The brick nogging is covered on the exterior with clapboards except on the front wall, where it is protected by a gallery and finished in plaster.

The detailing of the front gallery dates stylistically to the 1840s or 1850s and indicates that the present gallery has been remodeled or is an addition. The spacing of the front openings suggests that the original porch may have been a portico only as wide as the front door. An early rear gallery, enclosed at each end by the typical Natchez cabinet rooms, has been enclosed and extended. The dormers on the roof were added in the twentieth century.

The style of Hawthorne points to a construction date sometime in the 1820s or early 1830s when it was owned by the Overaker family. From 1825 to 1833 the land was the property of Maria Overaker, who may have been prompted to build the house by her 1830 marriage to Otasmus Nash. The style of the house does not rule out its construction by Robert Dunbar and family, who acquired the property in 1833.

HOLLY HEDGES

Having built a house on Lot 4 of Square No. 1 in the city and having no title, he asks grant to same. (Petition of John Scott to the Spanish Government, July 20, 1796)

Holly Hedges may be the same house built by 1796 when John Scott, a carpenter at the Spanish fort, was granted the property with the stipulation that he allow no bull fighting in the side yard. The house could also have been built about 1818, when the property was acquired by Edward Turner. The house appears in Audubon's 1822 landscape as a simple gable-roofed cottage, but Henry Tooley's 1835 landscape illustrates the house as it looks today after its enlargement by a rear addition with two distinctive gable roofs. Before this addition, Holly Hedges was arranged in the typical early Natchez manner with a short, narrow front hall set between two rooms and a wider, possibly open, back hall, or loggia, flanked by small cabinet rooms.

Holly Hedges is built close to the sidewalk and is entered through a Federal style doorway with an elliptical fanlight and sidelights decorated with hollow-sided diamonds. This finely detailed doorway is repeated on the interior at the back of the short front hall and at the back of the dining room addition. This repetition of fanlighted doorways is also found at Hawthorne and Fair Oaks.

Edward Turner, who bought the property in 1818, was mayor of Natchez from 1815 to 1819 and served Mississippi as state attorney, Speaker of the House of Representatives, and Chief Justice of the State Supreme Court. In 1832 Holly Hedges was deeded to Turner's daughter Mary and her husband John T. McMurran who later built Melrose. The beautifully detailed dormer windows were added to the house about 1950.

HOPE FARM

For one or more years, that well known situation, formerly the residence of Mrs. Overaker, within one mile of Natchez, on the Woodville road, called Hope Farm, containing about twenty-three acres of Land, with various kinds of fruit trees; a good Cistern and a never failing Well of water; a Dwelling House, with many useful and convenient out buildings. The extensive repairs, now in progress, will be completed, and possession given in all the month of November next.—The place can be examined by applying to W. Wren, Esq. the present occupant. (Southern Galaxy, November 26, 1829)

Hope Farm is probably the house that was purchased in 1789 by Don Carlos de Grand Pre, Commandant of the Natchez District, for his own residence. "Hospitality and Urbanity presided" there in 1791 when Don Carlos entertained his guest John Pope with "different Kinds of Fruits, Wines, and Parmesan Cheese, which were succeedent to very good substantial Dinner." As commandant from 1780 to 1792, Don Carlos laid out the present town of Natchez. His property was conveyed to George Overaker in an 1805 deed that refers to the estate as Hope Farm. Overaker operated a mercantile business in downtown Natchez and owned the White Horse Tavern at the foot of Homochitto Street. In 1835 ownership passed to the Montgomery family who owned the house until 1926 and gave it the predominantly Greek Revival character that remains today.

Hope Farm is a simple one-story frame house, three rooms across and two rooms deep, with a front gallery set under a low spreading roof that is gabled at one end and hipped at the other. The walls are covered with clapboard except on the front where plaster is scored to look like blocks of stone. At the rear, a two-story frame wing, built in two stages, is set at a right angle to the original one-story dwelling.

Hope Farm has become important during this century as the home of the late Katherine Grafton Miller, who is credited with the success of the Natchez Pilgrimage, one of the first organized house tours in America.

HOUSE ON ELLICOTT'S HILL

I was much struck with the similarity of Natchez to many of the smaller West Indian towns, particularly St. Johns Antigua, though not near so large as it. The houses all with balconies and piazzas. (Fortescue Cuming, Sketches of a Tour to the Western Country, *1810)*

The House on Ellicott's Hill, previously thought to be Connelly's Tavern, was built shortly after 1797, when the property was acquired by James Moore, a Natchez merchant. Ellicott's Hill is the site where, on February 27, 1797, Andrew Ellicott raised the flag of the United States in defiance of the Spanish authorities, who could see the flag from their position at Fort Rosalie on the southern end of the bluff promenade.

This National Historic Landmark house is significant for its early regional architecture, with a double-tiered front gallery, colonnettes on pedestals, and surrounding shed roofs attached high on a central gable roof. The architectural style of this house and numerous others similar to it caused two unrelated travelers in the first decade of the nineteenth century to compare Natchez to St. Johns, Antigua. This similarity in architectural character is understandable since Natchez and the West Indies were governed by the French, English, and Spanish and shared common trade interests as well as climate.

An unusual original interior feature of the House on Ellicott's Hill is the small plastered dome recessed into the ceiling of the parlor. Apparently, the practical function of this decorative dome was to restrict the amount of smoking on the ceiling from a candle or oil fixture. The restoration of this architecturally significant house by the Natchez Garden Club in the mid-1930s was the first building restoration project undertaken by an organization in Natchez.

The parlor of the House on Ellicott's Hill is well trimmed and has an unusual ceiling dome which concentrated most of the smoke from a ceiling fixture to decrease smoke damage to the ceiling. (*left*)

WILLIAM JOHNSON HOUSE

*I had the sheeting hauled down to the Building to day. The Rafters was put on yesterday and to day—the Brick Layers this Evening at work and will Finish or nearly do so tomorrow—I partly made a Bargain to Day with Mr Weldon to make me a pair of Dormer windows for Sixty Dollars. (*William Johnson's Natchez: The Ante-bellum Diary of a Free Negro, *October 9, 1840)*

The William Johnson House was completed in 1841 as the townhouse residence of barber William Johnson. A free black man, Johnson earned his place in American history by keeping a diary, which today provides historians with the most complete account of the life of a free black in the antebellum South. Johnson was born a slave in 1809 in Natchez and was granted his freedom in 1820, when his owner petitioned the state legislature, according to current law, to grant freedom to "the mulatto boy named William." Johnson's diary records the events of his day-to-day life, his successes and failures in business, and the happenings in Natchez, where almost half of the state's free black population resided. Johnson prospered in business, owned several properties and a few slaves.

William Johnson's house is a simple two-story brick building, originally constructed with shops below and living quarters on the second and third stories. The appeal of the Greek Revival house rests on its simplicity, its harmonious proportions, and the pleasing arrangement of windows and doors.

The William Johnson House was owned by the Johnson family until 1976, when it was purchased by the Natchez Garden Club, which realized its historic value and sought to protect it from commercial encroachment. In 1991 the National Park Service, United States Department of the Interior, acquired the house as part of the Natchez National Historical Park.

KING'S TAVERN

Probably the oldest house now existing in Natchez is the one occupied by Mrs. Postlethwaite, on Jefferson Street, between Union and Rankin. It was at one time kept as a tavern by a man named King, and was the stopping place of western men on their return from New Orleans, after selling out their flatboats of produce. (George Willey, early resident of Natchez, in Mississippi, As a Province, Territory and State, *by J. F. H. Claiborne, 1880)*

King's Tavern is generally believed to be the oldest building in the town of Natchez. Documentary evidence suggests that the building was built after 1794, when the Spanish government granted the lot to Prosper King. Early features of the house are its steeply pitched roof, the original beaded clapboards that have remained where they were protected by the side addition, and the exposed beaded beams in the large original room on the main floor.

King's Tavern is a two-story house, one room deep and one room across, with a one-story shed-roof porch at front and rear. A later side addition and rooms built under the porch increased the living space of the house. The raised basement may have been built when the street was cut through, a common practice described in nineteenth-century Natchez newspapers. King's Tavern was restored by the Pilgrimage Garden Club in the early 1970s and has been returned to its original function as a restaurant and tavern.

LANSDOWNE

My hunger was assuaged by Mr. Marshall, who drove me to his comfortable mansion through a country like the wooded parts of Sussex, abounding in fine trees, and in the only lawns and park-like fields I have yet seen in America. (William Howard Russell, My Diary North and South, *1863)*

Lansdowne, a modest mansion in the Greek Revival style, is a beautifully preserved and remarkably complete document of mid-nineteenth-century taste in architecture and interior decoration. Although only one-story in height, it is three rooms deep with the interior proportions and finish of a mansion. One of the grandest spaces in Natchez is the generous center hall that extends the entire depth of the house. On one side of the hall is a range of three bedrooms, and on the other side is a parlor, dining room, and pantry with original oak-grained cabinets. From the pantry, an enclosed stairway leads to a finished attic room, which is lighted by a high band of windows. The owners have always chosen to preserve the original furnishings, the marbleing and graining of the interior woodwork, and the outstanding parlor wallpaper, which features elaborate cut-out figures by Zuber and a background foliage paper by Delicourt dated 1853.

According to family tradition, Lansdowne was constructed in 1853 for George M. Marshall and his wife Charlotte, whose descendants still occupy the house. George was the son of Levin R. Marshall, a wealthy financier who lived at Richmond, and Charlotte was the daughter of Natchez planter David Hunt. Although his father was considered a Unionist or neutral, George Marshall served in the Confederate Army with the Natchez Southrons and was wounded during the Battle of Shiloh.

The front parlor at Lansdowne retains its original wallpaper, decorative painting, and furnishings. (*left*)

Lansdowne is a one-story Greek Revival residence with the finish and interior proportions of a grand mansion. (*right*)

LINDEN

This indenture made the seventeenth day of December in the year of our Lord one thousand eight hundred and forty-nine, Between John Ker and Mary Ker, his wife of the one part, and Jane E. B. Conner, of the other part . . . for and in consideration of Nineteen Thousand four hundred & thirty one Dollars . . . All that tract or parcel of land called "Linden," on which the said Ker has for some years resided. (Adams County Deed Book KK, December 17, 1849)

Linden is noted for the beauty of its richly detailed Federal style doorway and the grace of the long colonnade of its front gallery. In 1818, Thomas Reed, one of Mississippi's first United States senators, purchased a ten-acre tract where he "now and for some time past has resided." The earliest section built for Reed is the two-story central portion, consisting of a central hall with one room on each side and featuring an original two-tiered front portico. The interior is trimmed with delicate, gouge-carved millwork typical of the Federal period.

In 1829, Reed sold his residence, called Reedland, to Dr. John Ker. During Ker's ownership, galleried wings were added to each side of the house, the front wall was covered with lath and plaster to look like blocks of stone, the simple portico railings were replaced by turned balusters, and the balusters and columns of the portico were repeated across the front of the new wings. Jib windows provide access from the wing rooms to the long front gallery. A two-tiered back gallery and two rear wings create a pleasant, secluded courtyard edged by galleries on three sides. The two-story brick wing was the final addition and was added after 1849, when Dr. Ker sold Linden to widow Jane Conner, whose descendants still occupy the house.

LONGWOOD

Another Union family at Natchez were the Nutts. Mr. Haller Nutt was a millionaire when the war began. . . . "Longwood," the Nutt home, was about a mile and a half out of Natchez to the southeast on the Woodville Road. When the war began, it was in the process of being built anew. The blockade stopped its construction as the roof and first story were completed. The interior woodwork and furnishings, then at sea, never reached Natchez. This first story and the house for the servants, a good dwelling for any one, formed the Nutt abode in 1863. Many times we dined there. (Matilda Gresham, wife of the Union commander in charge of the occupation of Natchez, Life of Walter Quintin Gresham 1832–1895, *1919)*

The Civil War prevented the completion of Longwood, a National Historic Landmark constructed 1860–61. Also known as Nutt's Folly, Longwood is the largest and most elaborate octagonal house in America. Preserved in its incomplete state, the house gives silent and dramatic testimony to the impact of the Civil War upon the planting economy of the South.

Longwood was designed by noted Philadelphia architect Samuel Sloan for wealthy planter and physician Haller Nutt and his wife Julia, both natives of Mississippi. Probably having seen a design published by Sloan in 1852, Nutt engaged the architect in the late 1850s to design a similar house for his family in Natchez. Construction began in 1860 using skilled craftsmen sent by Sloan from Philadelphia. Work progressed quickly, and, in just over a year's time, the house was nearing completion. With the declaration of war in 1861, work on Longwood halted and the workmen returned home. Using local labor, Dr. Nutt completed the basement floor in a temporary fashion and moved his family inside the unfinished mansion to wait out the Civil War.

In June 1864, Haller Nutt died of pneumonia and his widow Julia was left alone to rear eight children in the unfinished mansion. Although she advertised at least twice for bids to complete Longwood, Julia Nutt died in 1897 in the basement of the unfinished house and was buried beside her husband in the Longwood family cemetery. Longwood was owned by the Nutt family until 1968 and is today maintained in its unfinished state as a house museum by the Pilgrimage Garden Club.

The millwork for Longwood was manufactured in Philadelphia and shipped to Natchez.

Although Julia Nutt twice advertised for bids to complete the house, Longwood remains unfinished to give silent testimony to the impact of the Civil War on the planting economy of the South.

Using local labor, Haller Nutt completed the basement story in a temporary fashion and moved his family inside the house to wait out the war. (*left*)

While the house was under construction, the Nutt family
68   lived in the servants' quarters to the rear of the great house.

MAGNOLIA HALL

Natchez, before the war, it appeared, had been the Bath or Clifton of the South, and the residences had more the appearance of wealth and style than those of any Southern city, with the exception of Charleston and New Orleans. They were the town residences of the planters, who owned large estates on the Mississippi, but who lived, for the most part at Natchez, as being more healthy than the low bottom lands of the river. The houses were mostly detached and really merited the name of family residences. They were solidly constructed of brick, covered in brown cement, resembling stone, and had massive columns, ascending from the front doorway to the top gable of the house, giving to it a majestic appearance, and affording also a delightful shade. (Therese Yelverton, Teresina in America, *1875)*

Magnolia Hall was probably begun in 1858 as the residence of Thomas Henderson, a Natchez native who became a wealthy cotton broker and merchant. The house was built on the site of the Henderson family home, Pleasant Hill, which was moved one block south to free the lot for the grander, more modern house.

The stuccoed walls are painted the color of the brownstone that was so popular in the Northeast during this period, and the scoring lines in the stucco are painted to resemble mortar. Unlike the other Natchez mansions, the staircase is located in the central hall rather than in a separate stair hall to the side.

The name of the house was inspired by the plaster magnolia blossoms incorporated into the design of the parlor ceiling centerpieces. Like its contemporary, Stanton Hall, Magnolia Hall has its kitchen located in an attached wing rather than in a detached outbuilding.

Magnolia Hall was restored and is operated as a house museum by the Natchez Garden Club.

MELROSE

. . . but surpassing all, that of Mr. McMurran, looking for all the world like an English park, ample mansion of solid design in brick with portico and pediment flanked by grand forest trees stretching away on either side, and half embracing a vast lawn in front of emerald green comprising at least 200 acres through which winds the carriage drive—The place is English all over. (Diary of architect T. K. Wharton, August 23, 1859)

A National Historic Landmark, Melrose is one of the best preserved and most significant historic sites in the entire South, unusually complete and well detailed, with a full array of outbuildings, a landscaped park, and formal gardens. The Greek Revival mansion was constructed ca. 1845 for Natchez attorney and Pennsylvania native John T. McMurran and his wife Mary. The designer and builder of Melrose was Jacob Byers, a Natchez architect and builder. According to Byers's 1852 obituary, he "made the plan and superintended the erection of the palace mansion of J. T. McMurran, Esq., by many considered the best edifice in the state of Mississippi."

In 1865, Melrose was acquired from the McMurrans by George Malin Davis, a wealthy Natchez attorney, who later gave the house to his daughter Julia upon the occasion of her marriage to New Yorker Stephen Kelly.

After his wife's death, Stephen Kelly located permanently in New York City, where his mother helped rear his only child, George Malin Davis Kelly. In 1900, George M. D. Kelly and his bride, Ethel Moore of New York, came to Natchez to see the holdings inherited from his mother's family. Kelly had inherited four Natchez mansions from the Davis family—Choctaw, Cherokee, Concord, and Melrose.

Mr. and Mrs. George M. D. Kelly decided to preserve and restore Melrose, and the house eventually became their permanent residence. Their decision to restore rather than remodel is remarkable, because the house was then only slightly more than fifty years old. After Mrs. Kelly's death in 1975, the house was sold intact with most of the furnishings, including the original parlor curtains and the painted canvas floorcloths of the front and rear hallways.

Because of the foresight of Mr. and Mrs. Kelly, who preserved and restored the house and because of the decision of their descendants and later owners, Mr. and John S. Callon, to sell the house almost intact, Melrose is today one of the most significant historic houses in America and is now owned by the National Park Service, United States Department of the Interior.

The master bedroom at Melrose is furnished with a rare pair of original canopied beds.

The front parlor at Melrose is trimmed with original window treatments and lighted by an original oil-burning, brass chandelier. The Rococo Revival furniture has been in the parlor since before the Civil War. Wide doorways with Grecian frontispieces link the range of three parlors.

The rear hall, or "saloon," as it was called in an 1865 inventory, has its original painted canvas floorcloth and oilburning ceiling fixture. Like most great Natchez mansions, the stairway is located in a separate side hall.

The focal point of Melrose's dining room is the magnificent mahogany ceiling punkah, or fly fan. The dining room furnishings are original.

The rear colonnaded gallery of Melrose opens onto a courtyard flanked by near matching two-story brick outbuildings,
latticed cistern houses, and brick privy and tool shed.

MISTLETOE

Mistletoe is a gem of a house, small in size and exquisite in detail. Its Federal style door is set beneath a half round fanlight and is flanked by lower sidelights to form a Palladian motif.

The two front rooms of Mistletoe are generously lighted by oversize windows and are set on either side of a short front hall. Two smaller cabinet rooms flank a wider and shallower rear porch which contains the stairs leading to the second floor.

The interior walls of Mistletoe are finished in flush cypress boards, and the trim is deeply molded in the Federal style, with corner blocks at windows and doors, molded panels on the mantel pieces, and molded chair rails and baseboards on the wainscots. A large room to the east, used for dining, was probably added to the house in the 1830s or 1840s. A windowed gallery across the rear and two flanking wings were added in the mid-twentieth century to create a private courtyard removed from the extensive grounds that surround the small plantation house.

Mistletoe was built as the residence of Peter Bisland on a portion of his father's Spanish land grant. The traditional family date for Mistletoe is 1807. The large windows, the rectilinear divisions of the sidelights, and the interior millwork, however, appear to date from the 1820s or 30s.

The house is still owned by members of the Bisland family.

76   Mistletoe is diminutive in size and exquisite in detail.

MONMOUTH

Auction. On Friday, the 7th day of January next, between the hours of 12 and 1 o'clock, wil be sold at the Vendue Office by virtue of a Deed of Trust, to the subscribers, the Estate known by the name of Monmouth, the former residence of John Hankinson, Esq. It is generally, esteemed one of the most eligible sites in the vicinity of Natchez; convenient for planters, merchants or professional gentlemen, having on it a handsome new brick dwelling house, with all necessary out houses, cistern, and large garden; all under good fence. (The Mississippi State Gazette, October 30, 1824)

Monmouth is one of the most severely monumental mansions in Natchez. The masculine strength of its design reflects both the forceful character of its most famous owner, General and Governor John A. Quitman, and the power of the Greek Revival style he chose for its ca. 1853 remodeling. The massive qualities of this style are evident on the facade where Quitman covered the original brick with scored stucco and built the large portico with its broad zigzag railing and its massive squared pillars. Monmouth's original Federal style interior trim includes carved, molded, and shaped overdoor panels and cornices and a gracefully curved stair.

Quitman's other additions include the east wing, the 1853 work of Cincinnati architect James McClure. This wing extends from the back corner of the house. Its two-story gallery wraps around the back of the main house. Quitman also added a second story and an arcaded gallery to the original brick kitchen.

Monmouth was built about 1818 for John Hankinson, an early Natchez postmaster who was a native of Monmouth County, New Jersey. The house was purchased in 1826 by attorney John Quitman, a native of New York who became one of Mississippi's most illustrious personalities. Elected to the state legislature in 1827, Quitman was appointed state chancellor and served until 1834, when he was elected to the state senate. His command in the Mexican War was the first to enter Mexico City upon its surrender. Elected governor of Mississippi in 1849, Quitman was an early secessionist and was opposed to the compromise measures of 1850. In 1855 he was elected to Congress for the first of two terms. Quitman was one of many victims of the "National Hotel disease" that hit Washington in 1857. Food poisoning was blamed for the mysterious deaths and illnesses, but some historians today believe that a form of Legionaire's Disease was responsible. Quitman lingered in ill health for months following his return from Washington and died at Monmouth in 1858.

78   Monmouth's central hallway is entered from the front and rear through half-round fanlighted doorways and contains a graceful stair that rises in a quarter turn from the rear of the hall.

MONTEIGNE

I made the last Union speech, I presume, that was made in the state of Mississippi. . . . My belief was that, some time or other, slavery would be the cause of war, and I wanted to postpone the evil day. I had been a colonizationist, and I hoped some means would be devised to rid us of slavery, because I never had any great fondness for the institution although I had been the owner of slaves from my youth up. . . . I came to Washington City and spent about a month here to see whether the war was inevitable, and if there was no way of avoiding it, . . . I made up my mind we had better make the best fight we could and go to work and get ready for it. . . . I went into it with all my heart and soul. (General William T. Martin, testimony before the Southern Claims Commission, December 12, 1877)

Monteigne was built in 1855 as the residence of William T. Martin, Natchez attorney and one of Mississippi's highest ranking Confederate generals. Martin, described by John R. Lynch, former slave and noted politician, as one of the most honorable men he had ever met, was an advocate of resettling slaves in Africa. An 1855 Natchez newspaper article informed readers about the construction of "a very spacious and beautiful cottage residence, now in the process of erection a mile from town, for W. T. Martin, Esq., . . . of which Mr. Jas. McClure is the architect and builder." McClure, who was the architect of the Greek Revival remodeling of Monmouth, had formerly been a Cincinnati architect. McClure designed and built Monteigne as an Italianate cottage with front and side galleries, but, in 1927 the New Orleans architectural firm of Weiss, Dreyfus, and Seiferth thoroughly remodeled the house in a neoclassical style. (Weiss, Dreyfus, and Seiferth also designed Louisiana's skyscraper state capitol and were the architects for the Eola Hotel in Natchez.) Monteigne's mid-nineteenth century origin is revealed on the interior in its doorway surrounds and mantel pieces and, on the exterior, in its side porches and side wing, which retains its original Italianate form and detailing.

The staircase in Monteigne's grand hallway dates to the 1927 remodeling but the doorway surrounds are original 1855. (*right*)

MOUNT REPOSE

Mount Repose is an unpretentious, Federal style plantation house that is simply decorated and well suited to answer to the necessities of antebellum life in the Southern climate. The double-tiered front galleries, which may be additions, provide cooling shade and allow windows to remain open for breezes during hot summer rains. Wide doorways at each end of the central hall provide maximum cross ventilation.

The first and second-story front doorways have oval fanlights and sidelights and the hall is decorated with delicate plaster ceiling molding nearly identical to the hall ceiling decoration at Rosalie (1823). A centerpiece of concentric circles is set within bands that edge the ceiling and curve inward at the corners to form circles. The central two-story section of the house is the oldest, and the flanking one-story wings were added after the Greek Revival style was introduced to Natchez in 1833. The hexagonal form of Mount Repose's original brick outbuilding, used at different times as kitchen, smoke house, and dairy, is unique for Adams County.

Mount Repose was built in 1824 as the residence of William Bisland and is one of three remaining pre-Civil War houses associated with the Bisland family of the Pine Ridge Community. Despite an 1866 advertisement for its sale, Mount Repose has always remained in the Bisland family.

Mount Repose's inviting bedroom is furnished with Bisland family furniture spanning several decades.

Monteigne was originally an Italianate cottage but was extensively remodeled in 1927 in a neoclassical style. (*left*)

MYRTLE BANK

The subscriber will sell low for cash, or approved short credit, ... her present residence on Pearl street known as "Myrtle Bank." The grounds consist of one undivided square, and are beautifully improved with every variety of ornamental shrubbery and shade trees. This property could be divided by the purchaser into lots, and sold as an advance; as a whole, forms a delightful residence combining the advantages of both city and country. . . . Ann D. Postlethwaite. (Natchez Daily Courier, January 12, 1856)

Myrtle Bank is a picturesque raised cottage located on an elevation that was called Myrtle Ridge in the nineteenth century. This ridge extended unbroken for several blocks, from the House on Ellicott Hill to beyond Myrtle Bank, until the streets were cut through the ridge in the early part of the nineteenth century. Recessed beneath the front slope of the roof is a full-width gallery that is accessed from each front room by jib windows, or windows set above moveable panels. Two rooms are located on each side of a wide central hallway containing a single-run staircase to the upper half-story. Construction probably began on Myrtle Bank shortly after 1836, when the property was acquired by Alfred Cochran and his wife Eliza, daughter of Samuel and Ann Dunbar Postlethwaite. Cochran died insolvent in 1837 and the house was purchased at public auction by Cochran's widowed mother-in-law. Ann Postlethwaite moved to Minnesota and sold the house in 1856 to Benjamin Wade. During the Wade family ownership, Myrtle Bank became home to the Natchez Young Ladies Institute operated by Mr. and Mrs. Charles Raymond. The basic form of the house dates to its construction in the 1830s, but the picturesque millwork of the front gallery and probably the gazebo in the front yard date to a significant early 1870s remodeling.

The two-story central section of Mount Repose was built in 1824, but the flanking one-story wings were added after the 1833 introduction of the Greek Revival style to Natchez. *(left)*

MYRTLE TERRACE

New Orleans, June 13—After surviving for sixty years all the perils to which steamboatmen are exposed, the world-renowned Captain Thomas P. Leathers is dead from the effects of being run over by a bicycle. One evening about four weeks ago he was crossing St. Charles avenue when a "scorcher" came along at high speed and ran into and knocked him down. The rider was also thrown down, but quickly remounted his wheel and made good his escape without being recognized. Captain Leathers never rallied from the shock. (The Daily Democrat, June 14, 1896)

Natchez builder Nathaniel Loomis Carpenter probably started building Myrtle Terrace for his own residence shortly after he purchased the property in 1844. He had not completed the house by 1851, however, when he sold it to Thomas P. Leathers in an "imperfect unfinished and dilapidated condition." Leathers was a Steamboat captain who piloted the *Natchez* in the famous race with the *Robert E. Lee*, the subject of a popular Currier and Ives print. As a condition of sale, Carpenter agreed to complete the house by June 1, 1851.

Carpenter built a house that was generously sized but modestly shaped like a regional cottage, with a large gable roof shading deep galleries at front and back. The ends of the back gallery were originally enclosed with the typical, small cabinet rooms. The slender columns of the front gallery are associated with the earlier Federal style and contrast with the large scale of the house and the bold, broad Greek Revival trim of the front doorway and the interior. The house derives its name from the terraced front yard and the abundant crepe myrtle trees. The beautifully landscaped yard is surrounded by a cast-iron fence in an elaborate Gothic pattern.

OAKLAND

In a week after they came to Natchez John Minor's house was a perfect hotel for officers, Generals & all; and remained so. John Minor told them that he expected they would have to send a guard out to keep his house, to keep the Confederates away. (Thomas H. Spain, testimony before the Southern Claims Commission, Washington, D. C., December 12, 1877)

Oakland is a one-story Greek Revival house that is distinguished by its grand interior proportions and fine architectural finish. Outstanding features of this suburban villa residence include beautifully molded woodwork, ornamental plaster, marble mantel pieces, and floor-length mahogany window sash with interior paneled shutters. The tall baseboards of the grand central passage are painted in imitation of sienna marble.

Oakland was constructed between 1838, when Catherine Chotard married, and 1844, when her father gave her the land "on which her husband Horatio S. Eustis has built a dwelling house." Eustis was a native of Rhode Island who came to Natchez after graduation from Harvard and was employed by Henry Chotard as a tutor for his daughter Catherine. In 1857, Eustis sold Oakland to his wife's cousin John Minor and his wife Katherine Surget, whose descendants occupied the house as late as 1949. John Minor was described by Julia Nutt of Longwood as "a very superior gentleman . . . [who] spent his life in fox-hunting and giving dinner parties, and reading literary works." During the Civil War, Oakland became significant as the center of Union sympathies in Natchez.

An unusual feature of Oakland is its mahogany window sash with interior paneled shutters. (*left*)

John Minor's Oakland was a "perfect hotel" for Union officers during the occupation of Natchez. (*right*)

THE PARSONAGE

On one of the most commanding sites upon Broadway, fronting the bluff and overlooking the river, a very spacious and well proportioned brick mansion has been built during the past few months on a beautiful spot, the donation of Peter Little Esq., and contiguous to his stately residence. It is the Parsonage of the Methodist Episcopal Church, and is now nearly completed—having a massive and substantial architectural appearance, overlooking the sweep of the mighty river for many miles from the cupola on the summit of the edifice. . . . At any rate, the style, execution, the size, admirable proportions and convenience of the mansion are alike creditable to the builders and to the church whose liberality has furnished the means to building so sightly a home for those who shall minister to them in holy things from generation to generation. (Concordia Intelligencer, April 3, 1852)

The main story of the Parsonage is raised on a full basement to provide a view over the edge of the bluff to the Mississippi River below. This imposing Greek Revival house features a wide, square-columned portico with a stucco finish that contrasts with the brick walls. The Parsonage has a back porch set between cabinet rooms and screened, not by the usual columns, but by a distinctive and beautiful arrangement of brick arches. The back porch connects with the gallery of an elongated post-Civil War wing that encloses one side of the back yard.

The Parsonage was constructed in 1852 by the Methodist Episcopal Church on land donated by Peter Little and located adjacent to his residence, Rosalie. The architect of the house was Natchez architect and builder James Hardie, a Scottish immigrant who came to Natchez in the early 1830s and became superintendent of construction for Neibert and Gemmell, a large antebellum contracting firm. The Methodist Church sold the Parsonage in 1865 to obtain a more conveniently located home for their minister. The house has been carefully preserved as a private home by the Metcalfe family since 1893.

An entrance doorway surrounded by colored glass opens into a spacious hallway at The Parsonage.

PLEASANT HILL

Mr. Alexander J. Postlethwaite, a ruling Elder in my church, died this evening at 10:30 o'clock after a lingering attack of typhus fever. He was one of the few truly righteous, whom we can ill afford to lose now. I mourn for him as a personal friend. I shall miss the clear shining of his Christian example. We needed his fervent spirit to stimulate our sluggishness. The wheat seems to be sifting out of our church and gathering into the garner in heaven. Are we to be left with only chaff? (Diary of Rev. Joseph B. Stratton, December 3, 1866)

Pleasant Hill is a wooden cottage that gains importance from its large size, its elevation upon a fully raised basement, and its high quality Greek Revival trim. The mass of the house is defined at the brick basement by a wide wooden base board and at the eaves by a simple Greek Doric entablature that wraps around the central front portico. The portico is supported at the wall by pilasters with molded panels and at the front by matching box columns. On the interior, a central hall, with a winding stair at the rear, separates the two rooms on each side. Across the back is the typical Lower Mississippi Valley arrangement of an open porch, now enclosed, with a small room, called a "cabinet," at each end.

Pleasant Hill was built about 1840 for the family of Natchez merchant John Henderson, whose son Thomas moved the house one block south in 1858 to clear the elevated site for his grander mansion, Magnolia Hall. Before and after the move, Pleasant Hill was the home of John Henderson's granddaughter and her husband, dry goods merchant Alexander J. Postlethwaite, in whose family the house remained until 1971.

PRESBYTERIAN MANSE

This will be a memorable day in the history of Natchez. Afternoon a boatload of Federal soldiers . . . came to our landing and proceeded to seize a quantity of ice. A party of people tumultuously started from the hill to attack them. They fired upon them as they were returning to their boat. . . . Immediately the ESSEX *and the transport opened fire upon the town, and from 3:30 o'clock to 6:30 the cannonading was kept up with little intermission. The population were thrown into terror. . . . The balls and shells were scattered pretty generally through the town and its is estimated that sixty-five houses were struck. In some instances the shell exploded within the dwellings which they entered. Yet, marvelous to record, but one life was lost, that of a little girl belonging to a family under the hill. . . . A fragment of a shell which exploded over us struck one of the buildings in my back yard. (Diary of Rev. Joseph B. Stratton, September 2, 1862)*

The Presbyterian Manse was probably built between 1824 and 1832 as the family residence of Mrs. Margaret Overaker, widow of George Overaker who operated the White Horse Tavern and lived at Hope Farm. In 1838, the trustees of the First Presbyterian Church purchased the property for a church parsonage. The small Greek Revival brick building in the side yard was built in 1849 as a study for the Rev. Joseph Buck Stratton, who was minister of the church from 1843 to 1893 and pastor emeritus from 1893 until his death in 1903.

Dr. Stratton's diary, which spans his sixty-year pastorate, provides one of the most comprehensive accounts of life in nineteenth-century Natchez. The Manse remains the home of ministers of the First Presbyterian Church.

91

RAVENNA

Know all men by these presents that I William Harris of the City of Natchez of the County of Adams and the State of Mississippi . . . do hereby give, grant, bargain, sell, . . . unto the Natchez Protection Insurance Company all that tract, piece, or lot of ground, situated in the City of Natchez, containing about fifteen acres being that part of a tract lying between two bayous . . . on which fifteen acre lot the said Harris is now building for a residence. (Adams County Deed Book X, April 7, 1836)

Ravenna was constructed in 1835–36 and is one of the earliest Greek Revival residences in Natchez. The form of the house is indigenous to the Lower Mississippi Valley with double-tiered galleries recessed under the front and rear slopes of the gabled roof. Although constructed during a transitional period when the Federal style was being replaced by the Greek Revival, Ravenna exhibits no trace of the earlier Federal style.

The matching front and rear galleries are supported by Doric columns on the first-story and by the higher order Ionic columns on the second-story. This sophisticated use of superimposed orders is known to exist at only one other Adams County residence, Brandon Hall. Outstanding architectural features of the house are the hallway arch supported by paired Doric columns and the elliptical staircase. This graceful staircase is entered at the rear of the hallway and continues to the third story with unbroken handrail. Ravenna was built by the Natchez contracting firm of Neibert and Gemmell for William Harris, a cotton commission merchant, real estate developer, planter, and Natchez alderman.

The hallway of Ravenna is elaborated by a hallway arch supported by paired Doric columns and a graceful elliptical staircase. (*left*)

The elliptical stairway at Ravenna spirals to the third story. (*right*)

Ravenna's two-story, double-tiered front and rear galleries are supported by Doric columns on the first story and Ionic on the second story.

RICHMOND

A few miles brought us to the superb estate of the Marshalls—passed through the entrance gates and rode up the long, sweeping, richly ornamented avenue to the mansion, which is palatial in extent and well designed. (Diary of T. K. Wharton, August 23, 1859)

Richmond is one of the great Natchez mansions where succeeding generations of the same family have preserved not only the house but also the outstanding interior Empire and Rococo Revival furnishings. Descendants of Levin R. Marshall, the wealthy financier who purchased the property in 1832, are responsible for making Richmond one of America's most important documents of mid-nineteenth-century taste in architecture and the domestic arts.

Richmond, constructed in three distinct stages, is one of the most unusual houses in Natchez. The center section was built first and may be the oldest structure in the Natchez vicinity. This early portion of the house is probably one of the two "wooden house [s] built in English manner" described as belonging to the late Juan St. Germaine in 1786, when an inventory of his estate was ordered by the Spanish government. Matilda Gresham, wife of Gen. Walter Gresham, commander of the Union occupation of Natchez, dined with the Levin R. Marshall family at Richmond and later wrote that construction began on the house in 1784, a date presumably told her by her hosts.

As originally constructed, the central portion was a one-and-one-half story frame house that might have rested upon a raised brick basement. The front and rear galleries are early additions, originally supported by enormous round columns made from solid logs. These later galleries obscure the massive hewn wooden gutters that originally carried rain water from the roof. The principal floor of this early central section underwent a Federal style remodeling in the early nineteenth century and a Greek Revival remodeling when the front section was added.

The front section, which is one of the most academically ambitious Greek Revival houses in Natchez, was built after the property was acquired in 1832 by Levin R. Marshall. The plainer, brick rear wing was the final addition made to the house before the Civil War.

Richmond's central hall features a curving staircase lighted by a skylight set into a saucer dome. (*right*)

Richmond is three houses in one with its Greek Revival
front section being one of the most academic expressions of
96   the Greek Revival style in Natchez.

ROSALIE

July 13, 1863, General Grant went to Natchez and made his headquarters in "Rosalie," the handsomest of the residences on the park I have just described. . . . Its lawns to the rear, the site of the old fort, and beyond were covered with tents [Union Army]. . . . Mrs. Wilson and her daughter, an only child, a demure miss whom our officers much respected, occupied all the upper part of the house except one of the front rooms, which was mine. Miss Wilson, then just out of school, was devoted to a Captain S. E. Rumble who was in the Confederate army. . . . All the lower floor except the dining room of General Grant was used for the executive offices. The dining room my husband and his staff used as their mess room. Mrs. Wilson and her daughter used one of the upper rooms as their dining room; their food was largely supplied by our mess. (Matilda Gresham, wife of the Union commander of the occupation of Natchez, Life of Water Quintin Gresham 1832–1895, 1919)

Rosalie is one of the great mansion houses of Natchez. From its position just north of the old French fort Rosalie, named for the Duchess of Pontchartrain, it overlooks the Mississippi River to the west and the old Spanish promenade along the bluff edge to the north. When Rosalie was constructed in 1823 for Pennsylvania native Peter Little and his wife Eliza, it apparently established an architectural form associated not only with the grand houses of Natchez but with plantation houses throughout the South. This mansion form consists of a hipped-roof two-story brick house with two-story high columns supporting both a portico that shelters the three central openings of the facade and a full-width gallery across the rear.

After Peter and Eliza Little's deaths in the 1850s, Rosalie was sold to Pennsylvanian A. L. Wilson. During the Wilson residency, the Federal style house underwent extensive interior redecoration which included the installation of elaborate plasterwork, marble mantel pieces, and over-mantel gilt mirrors. The Wilsons purchased in New York an eighteen piece set of Belter parlor furniture plus two centre tables and an étagère also attributed to the famous craftsman. The Belter parlor set has become so well known to scholars and collectors that Belter pieces of the same design are referred to as having the "Rosalie" pattern.

In 1938 the house was acquired from the Wilson heirs by the Mississippi State Society of the Daughters of the American Revolution, who today operate Rosalie as a house museum. The mid-nineteenth-century furnishings of the Wilson family remain in the house.

The four upstairs bedrooms at Rosalie feature original mid-nineteenth-century furnishings.

The double parlors of Rosalie are furnished with an eighteen piece Belter parlor set and original wall-to-wall Brussels carpeting. (*right*)

Rosalie is located on a high bluff overlooking the Mississippi River.

ROUTHLAND

For Sale. THAT DESIRABLE RESIDENCE, ONE MILE *from the city of Natchez, known as "Routhland,"* . . . *There are twenty acres of ground attached, highly ornamented and laid off in graceful beauty. The buildings have recently been put in thorough repair.* (The Natchez Daily Courier, July 7, 1860)

Routhland has undergone many remodelings since its construction and it exhibits characteristics of the Federal, Greek, and Italianate styles. The house was built as a Federal style cottage, with a central hall and two rooms to each side. The original, delicately molded woodwork survives in the rooms right of the entrance. The rooms on the other side were remodeled shortly before the Civil War to create an open arrangement of parlors separated by a columned arcade and trimmed with carved marble mantelpieces in the Italianate style. Other changes, including extensive additions at each end of the house and a large dining ell at the rear, had been made by the time of the Civil War. The central portico was extended in the mid-twentieth century to form a gallery across the front.

Routhland was built for John Routh between 1815, the year of his marriage to Nancy Smith, and 1824, the year that ten acres of land "including his house" were surveyed and laid off for John Routh from his father's property. Routhland is located on a portion of the 180-acre tract granted to Job Routh in 1794 and is the third house to be called by that name. The first Routhland was built in the late eighteenth century for Job Routh. This house burned in 1855 and was replaced on the same site by a second Routhland built as the residence of Job Routh's daughter Mary and her husband Charles Dahlgren. The name of the second Routhland was changed to Dunleith after the house was sold in 1859, at which time the present Routhland assumed the name. John Routh was described in a late nineteenth-century publication as having been the world's largest cotton planter in the early nineteenth century. After the Civil War, Routhland became the home of Charles Clark, Civil War governor of Mississippi.

The double parlors at Routhland were remodeled in the Italianate style about the time of the Civil War to create an open arrangement of parlors separated by a columned arcade.

SHIELDS TOWN HOUSE

*Free Trader Office Illuminated. On the last two working nights of last week, (thanks to Maurice Lisle, a most excellent Gas-fitter), an unusual flood of splendor was poured over our busy composition and press rooms. . . . In the composing room, half of the twelve burners shine more than a million of "dark lanterns," and are amply sufficient for all printing purposes. (*The Mississippi Free Trader, *November 29, 1858)*

Mr. and Mrs. Maurice Lisle began construction on their suburban Greek Revival residence probably shortly after they purchased the property in 1860. Like other Greek Revival houses built just before the Civil War, the house features Italianate details like columns atop pedestals, arched doorway panels, and an arched window in the pediment of the portico. The cottage-like exterior of the house belies its grand interior proportions. A spacious hall with graceful stairway extends the depth of the house to separate the parlor and dining room to the south from the library and bedroom to the north.

Maurice Lisle, a native of Delaware, operated a foundry business in Natchez, and his wife Isabella was the daughter of Natchez mayor John Stockman. Lisle expanded his foundry business to include the installation of gas pipes after gas lighting was introduced to the city in 1858. In 1869 the house was sold to the Wilmer Shields family, and it became known as the Shields Town House to distinguish it from the Shields country house on Oakland Plantation. The galleried wing with floor-length windows that extends from the northern side elevation was probably added by Shields shortly after he purchased the house. A brick kitchen and a brick office building with an interesting parapet facade are also located on the property.

SMITH-BONTURA-EVANS HOUSE (right)

THE UNDERSIGNED *offers for sale the desirable property, owned and occupied by him on Broadway. . . . The property embraces a good two story dwelling house, very recently built, extensive stables and carriage houses, kitchens, out buildings, &c. Robert Smith. (*The Daily Courier, *April 14, 1853)*

The Smith-Bontura-Evans House was built in the early 1850s as the residence of Robert Smith, a free black businessman of Natchez. Nearly half of Mississippi's free black population lived in antebellum Natchez, where Smith's residence is one of two surviving Greek Revival town houses constructed for substantial free black citizens.

Smith built for his home a simple unadorned brick town house, with a side stairhall and three rooms on each floor. The intricately patterned double-tiered cast-iron front porch was not added until the 1890s. Almost as large as the house is the two-story rear section where picturesque arched openings provided wide entrances for the carriages that Smith operated in his hack, or taxi, business. The two-story brick wing connecting the carriage house to the main residence is an addition, probably made about 1860 by Joseph Bontura, a Portuguese immigrant who adapted the house for use as an inn. Today Smith's residence is a house museum owned by the National Society of the Colonial Dames of America in the State of Mississippi.

JOHN SMITH HOUSE

SEXTON'S REPORT . . . *Deaths occasioned by the tornado of the 7th inst . . . John Smith. . . . DREADFUL VISITATION OF PROVIDENCE. About one o'clock on Thursday, the 7th inst., the attention of the citizens of Natchez was attracted by an unusual and continuous roaring of thunder. . . . The dinner bells in the large hotels had rung, a little before two o'clock, and most of our citizens were sitting at their tables, when, suddenly, the atmosphere was darkened, so as to require the lighting of candles. . . . In another moment the tornado, in all its wrath, was upon us. The strongest buildings shook as if tossed with an earthquake; the air was black with whirling eddies of house walls, roofs, chimneys, huge timbers torn from distant ruins, all shot through the air as if thrown from a mighty catapult. . . . In the upper city, or*

*Natchez on the hill, scarcely a house escaped damage or utter ruin. (*Weekly Courier and Journal, *May 16, 1840)*

John Smith was superintendent of construction for the antebellum contracting firm of Neibert and Gemmell, before becoming a partner in the firm in 1835. He probably designed and built his own residence shortly after he acquired the property in 1837. Smith died from injuries sustained in the devastating tornado that struck Natchez on May 7, 1840. The house was sold in 1852 at auction as part of the complex settlement of the estates of Neibert, Gemmell, and Smith, who had invested heavily in Natchez real estate and were financially ruined by the recession that followed the Panic of 1837.

The Smith-Bontura-Evans House was built about 1850 as the townhouse residence of free black Robert Smith. (*right*)

STANTON HALL

The edifice is an immense symmetrical brick pile. . . . All the mouldings, the arches that spring so gracefully over the halls, are carved from wood, and in a style that instantly arrests the attention and attracts intense admiration—the work of Mr. Saunders, after Lefevre's richest models. The magnificent white marble mantel pieces and jambs were sculpted in New York, and the immense mirrors were ordered from France. All the work on the edifice was done by Natchez architects, builders, artists and finishers. The grand front to the south presents a pure Corinthian facade, and might well be taken for a purely Grecian temple. On the eastern side another architectural style prevails—the tracery of the iron verandahs, closed alcoves and balustrades, strongly bringing to mind the Arabesque style of ornament. (Mississippi Free Trader, *April 5, 1858*)

Stanton Hall, the most palatial house in Natchez, is a National Historic Landmark noted for its grand scale, outstanding millwork, finely executed marble mantel pieces, French pier and over-mantel mirrors, and original gasoliers, which a publication on gaslighting describes as possibly the finest residential gas fixtures in America. The date of construction, 1857, is worked in plaster relief on the portico.

Probably designed by Thomas Rose, Stanton Hall, like many Natchez houses, was the product of local artisans, both black and white.

Like other Natchez houses constructed on the eve of the Civil War, the severe purity of the Greek Revival style is relieved by Victorian ornamental elaborations, some in the newly popular Italianate style. These decorative elements include the brackets and arched openings of the observatory and the lacy ironwork of the projecting bay to the side. A broad hallway, nearly seventeen feet tall, extends the seventy-five foot depth of the house. To one side is the stairway, occupying a separate hallway between the dining room and the library. To the other side is an unusual arrangement of three reception rooms, separated by sliding doors or hanging arches.

The town house mansion was the home of Irish immigrant Frederick Stanton, a planter and cotton merchant who originally named the house Belfast. Stanton died in 1859, not long after the house was completed, but his family remained there until 1894. For a brief time, the house was home to Stanton College for Young Ladies and the house name changed to Stanton Hall. In 1938, Stanton Hall was purchased by the Pilgrimage Garden Club who today open it as a house museum.

Stanton Hall has an unusual arrangement of three parlors, or reception rooms, separated by sliding doors or hanging arches. The marble mantel pieces were sculpted in New York, and the gasoliers have been attributed to Cornelius and Baker of Philadelphia.

The Stanton Hall dining room gasolier, which features Indians, corn, eagles, and oak leaves, is similar to gasoliers designed by Cornelius and Baker of Philadelphia for the United States Treasury Building in 1859.

Stanton Hall (down center) occupies an entire city block in downtown Natchez. The view from its observatory is a panorama of Natchez and the Mississippi River.

TEXADA

A LIVING ELEPHANT, *To be seen at Mr. Texada's large brick house, in this place, from Thursday the 18th to Wednesday the 24th inst. Those that wish to gratify their curiosity by seeing the wonderful works of nature, will do well to call previous to that time, as this is the only one in the United States, and perhaps the last visit to this place. Admittance 50 Cents—Children half price.* (The Weekly Chronicle, January 22, 1810)

Texada is a large brick building with a steeply pitched roof so distinctive that it is easily identified in John James Audubon's 1822 landscape of Natchez. Manuel Texada's house was the first brick building in town, according to an 1856 newspaper article, and possibly the finest building as well. The house is set close to the street on a corner in the old "Spanish Quarter" area of Natchez.

The simplicity of its substantial, solid, and imposing design is relieved by the original gabled dormers and delicate dentiled cornice and by the finely executed Federal style doorway that is original to Burling Hill, a demolished Natchez house attributed to Levi Weeks, architect of Auburn. The first floor, which features exposed beam ceilings, was not as finely finished as the upper two floors and was probably used commercially to house businesses like the American Eagle Tavern that advertised its location at Mr. Texada's. The upper floors probably constituted the principal living space until the house was remodeled in the mid-nineteenth century.

The exact year of Texada's construction has not been determined. In 1793, the Spanish government granted the lot to Michael Solibellas, and, in 1798, when the property sold at public auction to Manuel Texada, it contained a house fifty feet long and thirty feet wide including galleries. An 1806 newspaper advertisement noted that "Mr. Haughton's Dancing Academy Is now opened for the season in that Elegant Ball Room in Mr. Texada's new Brick House." In 1817, the house was purchased by Edward Turner, who served the city as mayor and became a state attorney general, Speaker of the Mississippi House of Representatives, and Chief Justice of the State Supreme Court. Before the state capital was moved from Natchez, the state legislature assembled at Texada.

A picturesque fence encloses the rear courtyard at Texada.

The first story of Texada, which features exposed beam ceilings, was not as finely finished as the upper two floors and was probably used commercially when the house was new.

Texada was the first brick house constructed in Natchez.
(*right*)

THE TOWERS

On the following pages will be seen Plans of Forty-five BRICK, STONE, *and* FRAME BUILDINGS, *for which Hinkle, Guild & Co. have furnished all or part of the Wood Work, with the Location, Name of Owners, Architects, Superintendents, and Builders. . . .* RESIDENCE OF W. C. CHAMBERLAIN, NATCHEZ, MISS. J. EDWARD SMITH, *Architect, Natchez, Miss. (Catalogue of Hinkle, Guild & Co., Cincinnati, Ohio, 1862)*

The rich Italianate facade of the Towers was built on the eve of the Civil War as a new front to an earlier frame cottage. The new front included a two-story recessed porch, or loggia, with three arches on each floor, set between matching three-story towers that were the source for the name of the house. The third stories were lost to fire in the 1920s.

J. Edwards Smith, a local attorney, was the architect for the Towers as well as for Zion Chapel A.M.E. Church in Natchez and Christ Church at neighboring Church Hill. The house was built for W. C. Chamberlain, probably shortly after he acquired the property in 1859. The house was sold in 1861 to Mr. and Mrs. John Fleming, whose descendants now own the property that had been out of the family for about fifty years. During the Union occupation of Natchez, the Towers was located within Fort McPherson, a large earthwork fortification constructed in the northern suburbs of town. Union Officers occupied the house while soldiers pitched tents on the eight acres of landscaped grounds.

TWIN OAKS

*On Saturday, the 7th day of April next, at the door of the Court-house, in the city of Natchez. . . . will be sold that beautiful and valuable property, late the residence of C. L. Dubuisson, Esq., on the northwardly side of Homochitto street, in the suburbs of the city. This property contains about 12 acres, more or less; a good and elegant brick dwelling, nearly new, built in modern style, with four large rooms, besides closets, &c., attached; comfortable bedrooms in the attic; and a frame building with several rooms in the rear; all connected by large and commodious galleries; several out-buildings, and cisterns. Many valuable fruit trees and shrubbery, add to the comfort and value of the property, while its proximity to Natchez, give it the advantages of both a city and country residence. (*Natchez Daily Courier, *March 19, 1866)*

Twin Oaks is a story-and-a-half Greek Revival house that gains distinction from the imposing, temple-like portico that adorns the facade. A deep cornice caps the front wall and extends around the broad portico where it appears to be supported by sturdy square columns. A half-round window lights the gable of the portico and dormer windows light the rooms of the upper half story.

Stylistic and documentary evidence indicates that Twin Oaks was built in 1852 by contractors Thomas Bowen and John Crothers, who, alone and in partnership, built several Natchez buildings in the Greek Revival style, including Dunleith, the Catholic Rectory, the William Ailes House, and Sunnyside. The house was constructed as the residence of Charles Dubuisson, a native New Yorker who contributed significantly to education and law in Natchez. Dubuisson came to Natchez in the early 1830s to become a professor at Jefferson College, the first state-chartered institution of higher learning. He became president of the school in 1835 and organized the Jefferson College and Washington Lyceum during his tenure. Dubuisson later practiced law in Natchez and became a judge of probate court.

WEYMOUTH HALL (right)

Among the many beautiful private residences in the process of erection or completion, that of Judge Reuben Bullock, deserves particular notice. It is situated on the brow of one of the hills immediately above the United States Marine Hospital, and from it is to be enjoyed one of the finest views of the Mississippi River and its valley, that can be any where obtained. . . . The view commands several miles up and down the river, reaching into Louisiana, far beyond Lake Concordia, and overlooking the magnificent plantations with their fields, woods and white-washed cottages and quarters, which occupy the opposite parish. The house itself is one of great beauty and convenience in its arrangement, and well deserves a visit. . . . we were especially struck with the beauty and excellence of the plastering. . . . The walls are hard-finish, beautifully ornamented, and as clear, brilliant and perfect in the color, as could possibly be desired. The entire lower part of the house is laid with cement floors, finished to resemble polished stone. (The Natchez Daily Courier, June 9, 1855)

The cubical mass, clean lines, and spectacular siting of Weymouth Hall make it one of the most impressive Greek Revival mansions in Natchez. The house has matching river and land facades with loggias (recessed porches) that command spectacular views of the Mississippi River to the west and the landscaped Natchez City Cemetery to the east. Constructed near the edge of the high river bluff, the house is further elevated upon a fully raised basement.

The interior rooms are arranged in an "H" plan with a large central room forming the cross bar of the "H" on both levels of the house. The central room of the principal floor opens onto both front and rear loggias through a central doorway flanked by floor-length windows to create a room with unequaled scenic vistas and cross ventilation. A hallway separates the two northern rooms of each floor and contains the staircase, which runs with unbroken handrail from the basement to the clerestory room at the peak of the roof.

Weymouth Hall was constructed in 1855 as the residence of Judge Reuben Bullock and his wife Sarah, a niece of Mrs. John Weymouth who resided with the Bullock family after the death of her husband in 1852. The house was built on property long owned by John Weymouth and inherited by his wife's niece. Missing from the house is the original one-story gallery with railed roof that completely encircled all elevations of the house and is documented in Civil War era photographs.

VAN COURT TOWN HOUSE

Josephine Quegles Ferguson   *died May 1, 1837 age 23*
Joseph Quegles Ferguson   *April 12, 1834–December 3, 1836*
William Brune Ferguson   *December 6, 1835–January 17, 1836*
James Ferguson   *March 10, 1837–May 10, 1837*
                (Natchez City Cemetery)

Natchez has been . . . associated with miasma and marshes. . . . Pestilence has here literally "walked at noonday" . . . converting the green earth into a sepulchre. (Joseph Holt Ingraham, The South-West. By a Yankee, 1835)

The Van Court Town House was constructed in the mid-1830s, when Natchez architectural fashions were slowly changing from the delicate Federal style to the robust but chaste Greek Revival style. Both styles are blended in a single building at the Van Court Town House, where a graceful oval fanlight in the Federal style crowns the front door which is framed by Grecian pilasters. The lacy cast-iron porch was probably added in the 1850s. The rooms are arranged in a side hall plan with a graceful hallway staircase extending, with unbroken handrail, from the first to the third story.

The Natchez contracting firm of Neibert and Gemmell built the Van Court Town House for James Ferguson, shortly after he purchased the property in 1834. This corner lot was part of the estate of his father-in-law, Joseph Quegles, a prominent early Natchez merchant and planter. Ferguson's wife and three children had died by 1838, when Ferguson sold the house to Dr. Andrew McCrery. The house received its name from yet another owner, Dr. Elias J. Van Court, who purchased the house in 1882.

WIGWAM

Know All Men by These Presents, That I Eliza L. Rivers widow of the City of Natchez . . . have this day granted, bargained and sold . . . all that lot or parcel of ground . . . containing seven acres, more or less, Known as the "Wigwam," and being the place of residency of myself and family. (Adams County Deed Book WW, December 30, 1879)

Wigwam's Italianate front, with wings that project forward on either side of the front porch to create an entrance loggia, was built just before the Civil War as an addition to the front of a large cottage dating to about 1836. The arched triple windows, the large central dormer, the bracketed cornice and the cast-iron porch posts and railings are all part of the Italianate remodeling that originally included balconies that wrapped around the projecting wings. The western wing room is noted for its painted ceiling, divided into geometric spaces, each further elaborated with painted moldings, foliage, and flowers. This painted decoration was probably the work of D. W. Ducie, an ornamental painter. Elaborate plaster work, marble mantel pieces, and arched doorways with deeply molded trim are other elements of the lavish remodeling.

The Wigwam was built on a portion of the Cottage Gardens property that was sold in 1836 to four sisters—Margaret, Matilda, Laura, and Amanda Ivey. Laura Ivey referred to the property in her 1841 will as the "River View Estate consisting of a House and grounds." In 1858 the property became the home of Mr. and Mrs. Douglas Rivers, who apparently commissioned the remodeling and named the house the Wigwam. Mrs. Rivers, the former Eliza Little, was the adopted daughter of Mr. and Mrs. Peter Little of Rosalie. During the Civil War, the Wigwam was located within the boundaries of Fort McPherson, the Union fortification in the northern part of the city, and was occupied by Union army officers.

Index